THE INVESTIGATION
OF
MIND IN ANIMALS

MONKEY PERFORMING PLUG EXPERIMENT

a, slide door giving access to food, which could be obtained when the monkey by pulling the string, *b*, passing through a hole, *c*, removed the plug, *d*.

THE INVESTIGATION

OF

MIND IN ANIMALS

BY

E. M. SMITH

Moral Sciences Tripos, Cambridge

Cambridge:

at the University Press

1923

CAMBRIDGE
UNIVERSITY PRESS

University Printing House, Cambridge CB2 8BS, United Kingdom

Published in the United States of America by Cambridge University Press, New York

Cambridge University Press is part of the University of Cambridge.

It furthers the University's mission by disseminating knowledge in the pursuit of education, learning and research at the highest international levels of excellence.

www.cambridge.org
Information on this title: www.cambridge.org/9781107626560

© Cambridge University Press 1923

First edition 1915
Second edition 1923
First published 1923
First paperback edition 2013

A catalogue record for this publication is available from the British Library

ISBN 978-1-107-62656-0 Paperback

PREFACE

THERE are few people who cannot relate some apparently striking instance of animal intelligence; the majority of such cases, however, will not stand critical examination. The science which has for its object the systematic investigation of the brute mind is Animal Psychology, and it would seem that the methods of this youthful discipline are still unknown to many, even among those who profess an interest in animal conduct. It is, then, with the purpose of presenting a brief account of the modes of procedure employed by Animal Psychology, its aims, trend, and the general nature of the results hitherto obtained, that this little book has been written. In a work of this character discussion and controversy would have been out of place, so the treatment has been confined as far as possible to description and illustration; at the same time attention has been drawn to some of the chief difficulties inherent in the inquiry. A complete and exhaustive presentation of facts was, of course, out of question, and much that is of interest and importance has had, inevitably, to be omitted; but it is to be hoped that the interested reader of leisure will refer to some, at least, of the original articles mentioned in the bibliography, nearly all of which will be found to contain further references.

For permission to reproduce the various figures I am indebted to the courtesy of the following: to the Columbia University Press for figures 1 and 3 (from Jennings, *Behavior of the Lower Organisms*), to the Macmillan Company for figures 4, 6 and 9 (from Washburn, *The Animal Mind*, Yerkes, *The Dancing Mouse*, Thorndike, *Animal Intelligence* respectively); to Professor R. W. Yerkes for figures 2 and 7 (from the *Journal of Animal Behavior*); to Professor G. Stanley Hall for figure 5 (from the *American Journal of Psychology*); to the Houghton Mifflin Company for figure 8 (from Peckham, *Wasps, Social and Solitary*); and to the Wistar Institute of Anatomy and Biology for the frontispiece (from the *Journal of Comparative Neurology*).

I desire to express my grateful acknowledgment of the help and advice received from Dr C. S. Myers, who most carefully read through both manuscript and proofs, making many valuable suggestions to the great improvement of the text. To Mr C. L. Burt, who kindly read through the proofs, I am indebted for numerous emendations. My thanks are also due to Miss C. M. Ryley, whose friendly criticism has helped to remove much that was obscure or confused in expression. Lastly, I must thank Mr J. T. Cunningham for permitting me to consult him at considerable length on the subject of hormones, and their possible *rôle* in inciting to functional activity the periodic instincts.

It only remains to state that for all errors, whether of fact, exposition, or interpretation, I alone am responsible.

E. M. S.

Cambridge,
March, 1915

PREFACE TO THE SECOND EDITION

THE call for a second edition of *Mind in Animals* has rendered a certain amount of revision necessary. To incorporate the results of the numerous papers bearing on the subject of Animal Behaviour which have been published since 1914 would have meant adding greatly to the size of the book, and as the majority of these contributions revolve round difficult questions of technique, or are somewhat controversial in nature, discussion of them would not have been in place in a short introduction to the subject.

One section, however, deals with entirely new matter. The final section of the first edition, which gave an account of the famous 'talking' horses, I have decided to omit from the present edition, and to replace it by a discussion of the Multiple Choice method of Yerkes and the method of studying perseverance reactions devised by van Hamilton. As yet these methods have not been widely applied, but it is to be anticipated that they will be considerably developed and extended in the future.

For the rest the alterations in the text are chiefly verbal in character. Certain additions have been made to the bibliography.

I desire to express my indebtedness to my husband, Mr F. C. Bartlett, for his help in preparing this new edition for the press.

My thanks are also due to the Syndics of the Press for their courtesy in permitting the aforesaid alterations.

E. M. B.

CAMBRIDGE,
  October, 1922

CONTENTS

ILLUSTRATIONS

CHAPTER I

UNLESS we set out with the preconception
that mind is the prerogative of man, the question whether mind is coextensive with living
protoplasm or is the possession of only the more
highly organized animals must at some time
suggest itself. But, whatever prejudices we may
hold, it is incumbent upon us, before definitely
accepting either view, to ascertain, if possible,
the level at which the first manifestations of
mind occur. On either finding, too, it is of the
utmost importance for our proper comprehension
of the developed mind to trace its gradual evolution from the simpler to the more complex forms ;
and, furthermore, the study of mental phenomena
at the earliest stage of their appearance helps to
demonstrate the more primitive, fundamental,
and inalienable characteristics of mind.

The solution of these and kindred problems
cannot be decided *a priori*, but demands the

careful study and systematic observation of the behaviour of different organisms under widely varying conditions ; and to this study much labour and ingenuity have been devoted during the past few decades. It is the aim, then, of this essay to present briefly certain of the more important evidence yielded by these investigations.

In view of the importance attaching to the first appearance of mind in the animal kingdom, it will be well at the outset of our survey to give some account of what is now known of the habits and behaviour of the structurally simplest animals, the Protozoa. It will be clearer and more convenient to confine our attention as far as possible to one class of these minute creatures. We will, therefore, select for our purpose the ciliate infusorian *Paramecium*, since its reactions may, in many respects, be regarded as representative of the more typical features of protozoan conduct, and are illustrative of the main points to be presented.

The most outstanding feature of a *Paramecium's* behaviour consists in its definite and well-marked reactions to certain chemicals. For instance, if a drop of weak sulphuric or proprionic acid be introduced, by means of a

capillary pipette, into a slide of *Paramecia*, the
animals will quickly collect within the region of
the acid, and, forming a dense aggregation, will
remain there.   Similar behaviour may also be
shown towards certain injurious chemicals : thus,
Paramecia freely swim into a drop of corrosive
sublimate, only to encounter instant death.
Numerous other conditions could be cited which
elicit this aggregation phenomenon, notably a certain optimal degree (which varies with adaptation)
of warmth ; but the instances already given must
suffice for illustration.

Equally striking, on the other hand, is the
marked distaste and avoidance normally shown
by these animals towards certain other conditions, among which may be mentioned a solu-
tion of common salt from $\frac{1}{10}$ per cent. upwards,
extreme heat, and light containing ultra-violet
rays ; the areas where these conditions obtain
being completely deserted.   The introduction of
any of these stimuli is accompanied by a well-
marked dispersal phenomenon which contrasts
strongly with the aggregation phenomenon referred to above.

From these and like observations Loeb was
led to conclude that the lower organisms are
mere automata, certain stimuli attracting them

with a fatal inevitableness, as a magnet attracts steel, while others no less certainly repel them. Of such simple, direct, irresistible and automatic responses Loeb conceives protozoan conduct to consist; and, on account of its analogy with certain facts in plant life, long known as tropisms, his view is commonly referred to as the 'tropistic' theory.

Another worker, Jennings, however, not content with thus recording only the end-state of the *mass* effect caused by these various stimuli, sought to observe precisely in what manner and by what processes this end-state was brought about. To do so it was necessary to scrutinise closely the behaviour of *individuals* from the moment of the first disturbance caused by the test stimulus until such time as a state of apparent equilibrium was reached. And so important are the results yielded by this minute examination that some account must now be given of them.

On observing individuals closely, it was found that when a drop of a weak acid solution was introduced, as already described, into a slide of *Paramecia*, the animals still continued swimming restlessly about in their usual random and aimless manner; but that when *by chance* any

individual came into contact with the drop
of acid solution, such individual entered and
remained there, its activity thenceforward being
confined within the boundary of the acid.
Gradually, through their active exploration,
all or the greater part of the *Paramecia* encounter the acid, and so a dense aggregation
comes to be formed. So far it should be noted
that the acid exerts no *direct* attraction on the
organisms, which after its introduction swim
about in a random manner in all directions,
only being brought into contact with the acid
by chance.

The next point of interest is to consider
how the acid succeeds in acting as a trap. In
order to understand this some account of the
structure of a *Paramecium* must be given.

A *Paramecium* is a ciliate infusorian supposed
to resemble a slipper in shape, and on that
account sometimes spoken of as the slipper
organism (see fig. 1, p. 7). Its body is entirely
covered with fine hair-like structures or cilia set
in oblique rows. In swimming the animal is
carried forward by the backward movement of
the cilia ; retreat is accomplished by a reversal
of the ciliary wave. Both movements, however,
are accompanied by a slight rotation on the

long axis, caused by the fact that the cilia
are set obliquely.   Further, one side of the
organism is differentiated by bearing the oral
groove, a long funnel extending from the mouth,
in the middle of the body, forward to the anterior
end. Owing to the fact that the cilia in the oral
groove beat rather more strongly than the rest
the anterior end is continually being turned
away from the oral side.   An admirable instance
of these movements is to be seen in *Paramecium's*
reaction to an obstacle (fig. 1).   *Paramecium*, on
the whole, tends, except in certain physiological
states, to avoid contact with large, solid bodies.
Its behaviour may be roughly described as
follows :—One of these infusoria on coming into
contact with *débris* or other objects stops suddenly, reverses the stroke of its cilia thus causing
a backward movement, then pausing, turns aside,
and once more starts on a forward course, thereby
completing the sequence of movements known
as the 'motor reflex' or 'avoiding reaction.'
If the new direction also brings it into contact
with the obstacle, a fresh avoiding reaction is
given, this behaviour being, for a time, repeated
on each contact with the obstacle.   Sooner
or later the combination of the backward movement with the summation of turns toward the

aboral side tends to bring the animal into a direction facing a clear path where it may swim forward unimpeded for the moment. A diagrammatic representation of this behaviour is given below in fig. 1.

We are now in a position to understand how the aggregation phenomena, so frequently

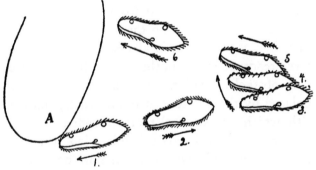

Fig. 1 Diagram of the avoiding reaction of *Paramecium*. *A* is a solid object or other source of stimulation. 1-6, successive positions occupied by the animal. (The rotation on the long axis is not shown.) (After Jennings.)

observed in the behaviour of these organisms to certain stimuli, are brought about. To return to the *Paramecia* caught (by mere accident as we have shown), in the drop of weak acid, close attention to their movements will show that the individuals which have entered this drop are frequently very active, swimming about within it restlessly in every direction. The sole uniform feature which their conduct presents consists in the ' motor reflex ' (constituted, as we have just seen, of a backward movement followed by a sharp turn) which is invariably given by each animal on arriving at the margin where acid and water meet. By this reaction the animals are prevented from re-entering the water and are kept within the region of the acid. Their behaviour here is in all essentials similar to that already described in the case of the avoidance of an obstacle, the obstacle in this instance being replaced by the different medium, water, contact with which occasions the motor reflex.

The true explanation underlying the so-called ' tropistic ' responses will now be readily understood. The attraction of weak acids and of the cooler region is shown on closer observation to be apparent rather than real. It is a negative and not a positive phenomenon, being ultimately due to avoidance of the adjoining conditions. And this avoidance does not occur in a definite and immediate manner but is only achieved, if at all, by a process of trial. The avoidance of extreme heat, of salt solution, and of ultra-violet rays is to be similarly explained. These unfavourable conditions arouse the animal to increased restlessness, until it finally passes out of the area of stimulation : no specially marked reaction occurs on passing out of this region ; but should the animal in the course of its activity again encounter the objectionable stimuli, the avoiding reflex is repeated, and so the unfavourable area remains deserted.

The significance of the difference between the two theories of interpretation of the behaviour of the lower organisms—the one just described which will be referred to as the ' trial and error ' interpretation, and the tropistic theory previously dealt with — will now be evident. Whereas the latter theory requires that the organisms shall respond to significant stimuli with a fatal inevitableness and immediacy, the trial and error hypothesis involves, potentially at least, the testing of conditions over a relatively wide area by the animals. Thus, *Paramecium*, as we have just seen, in avoiding an unfavourable region tries various directions, and only comes to rest when fatigued, or on meeting with conditions adapted to its requirements. On the occurrence of any changes, either in the internal condition of the animal or in the external conditions of the environment, such as render the latter no longer suited to the former, the animal once more swims away, testing different directions until again satisfied. Similarly, movements tending to take it out of the favourable area are corrected. In short, the facts brought out by the detailed observations upon which the trial and error theory is based, show that emphasis must be laid not so much on the intrinsic character of external stimuli as on the changes which occur in accustomed conditions. And such changes need not necessarily consist in the substitution or introduction of a novel stimulus. A mere variation in the intensity of the stimulus often suffices to effect a reversal of behaviour; a fact which is utterly at variance with the tropistic interpretation. This change of reaction consequent upon alteration in the intensity of the stimulus is usually known as sensibility to difference.

The importance of the *rôle* assumed by a change in accustomed conditions leads to a consideration of the phenomenon of adaptation or acclimatization.

It has long been known that if one hand is placed for a few seconds in water heated to about 40° C. and then transferred to water the temperature of which is approximately that of the skin (30° C.), immersion in the latter, which as a rule evokes no pronounced temperature sensation, will now occasion a distinct sensation of cold. Moreover, the hand can bear immersion in water heated to a rather higher degree than usual if subjected immediately before to immersion in water heated to 40° C. Facts such as these are closely paralleled in the life of the Protozoa. For example, *Paramecium* as a rule gives the avoiding reaction to weak saline solution and to all degrees of temperature below 24° C. or above 28° C. But if kept for some time in $\frac{1}{10}$ per cent. salt solution or at a temperature of 36°–38° C., it will be found that the optimum has temporarily changed and that the avoiding response will no longer be given to weaker salt solution or to temperatures of from 30° to 32° C., but only to relatively strong salt solutions, and to temperatures higher than 32° C. or lower than 30° C.

The problem now arises as to why conditions which at one time are consistently avoided at another should evoke no response. The explanation which most readily suggests itself is that subjection to a stimulus of a certain intensity blunts discrimination in regard to lesser degrees of intensity of the same stimulus.

That blunting of discrimination does occur is evident from the facts recently recorded in regard to the selection of food by the organism *Stentor*. Schaeffer has found that whereas this animal, when nearly satiated, nicely discriminates between *Trachelomonas* and *Euglena*—consistently rejecting the former—it, nevertheless, manifests no such preference in a more hungry condition. Thus, if a mixture containing the two organisms in question together with starch, grain, sand, etc., be offered to a hungry *Stentor*, the animal while still rejecting the starch and sand, etc., will now swallow *Trachelomonas* with an avidity equal to that shown for *Euglena*.

But this explanation does not reach the root of the matter ; for behind both acclimatization and the various grades of discrimination there lies what may be termed the inner condition or physiological state of the organism. This state is undergoing continuous change according as the animal is hungry or replete, fresh or fatigued, injured or whole, etc. ; and these changes which take place in the physiological state of an organism are every whit of as great an importance in determining activity as are the various external stimuli to which the animal

is subjected. It is not sufficient to regard
an organism's behaviour in the manner of the
tropistic theory, as being solely composed of a
sum of specific responses (together with their
mutual interactions) to various stimuli. Such
a view ignores the nature of the organism as a
vital unit. And not only so, but it fails to
explain a fact conclusively demonstrated, namely,
that the same stimulus may, at different times,
elicit diverse responses from an individual. It
follows that an infusorian's conduct cannot be
predicted so readily as was once believed, since
the nature of its activity at any moment is not
a simple function of certain specific external
stimuli, but is largely determined by the physiological condition which in turn is the outcome of
its past states. The series of reactions given by
Paramecia to filter paper may be taken as an
instance. These animals on coming into contact
with a small piece of filter paper first give the
usual avoiding reaction. It has been observed,
however, that, should this response not prove
successful, subsequent contact may again occasion the avoiding response, though this time in
a less marked manner—the backward movement
being greatly reduced. If this further reaction is
also unsuccessful in evading the obstacle, the

Paramecium may finally settle against the paper,
—passing on after a few seconds to a new position,
but still in contact with the paper. Finally it
leaves the paper and swims away. As Jennings
remarks : ' So far as can be seen, the Paramecium first responds to the solid by the avoiding
reaction, later by the positive contact reaction,
and still later suspends the contact reaction,
all without any change in external conditions.
The changes inducing the change in reaction
must then be within the animal.'

In other organisms, *Peranema* and *Stentor*,
we also find a well-defined series of different
responses resultant upon a single stimulus.
In the case of the former animal, a flagellate,
it has been found that when a specimen becomes
entangled in a fibrous mass, the following
sequence of actions occurs. (*a*) Not only the
tip of the flagellum, as under normal conditions,
but a much greater part becomes active, beating
backwards and forwards with increased vigour.
If this response is unsuccessful in freeing the
animal from the obstruction it is followed by
(*b*) a sharp turn of the body and swimming
away in the new direction (fig. 2). These
reactions may be rapidly alternated until *Peranema* is freed from the *débris*.

In the classical instance of *Stentor* the variety
of responses is greater. *Stentor* is a small trumpet-
shaped ciliate. The lower portion of its body
is enclosed in a sheath or tube formed from a
mucous secretion. At its smaller end, known
as the foot, the protoplasm throws out pseudo-
podia by means of which the animal attaches
itself to some water-plant or *débris*. If an

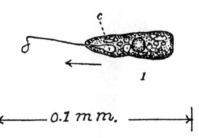

Fig. 2. *Peranema* crawling in the direction of the arrow ; only
the bent tip of the flagellum is active. (After Mast.)

irritating substance, such as finely powdered
carmine, be dropped on the oral disc of the
extended animal, *Stentor* may, at first, appear
indifferent, engulfing the particles in the usual
manner (fig. 3). If the stimulation be continued,
however, the animal generally bends over towards
the aboral side, a reaction which may be repeated
several times. When this mode of response

is inadequate to free the animal from the foreign substance, it is frequently succeeded by one totally different—the action of the peristomial

Fig. 3.   A cloud of carmine is introduced into the water currents passing to the mouth of the *Stentor*.   (After Jennings.)

cilia surrounding the oral disc is for a moment reversed, a response adapted to throw particles off the disc.   Should this in turn prove inadequate, more vigorous measures are resorted to. *Stentor* strongly contracts its whole body, then, slowly, extends again. And, finally, if the stimulus still persists, the contractions increase in vigour and rapidity. This measure generally results in freeing the creature from its attachment. Thereupon it swims away to seek a more congenial neighbourhood.

It will be evident from these few examples that the internal physiological condition of an organism is an important factor to be reckoned with in calculating an animal's responses to its environment; and, further, that the *rôle* played by internal conditions is adaptive and regulatory, accommodating the animal to deal with a particular environment in a manner more effective for its welfare. Thus, *Stentor's* responses to an irritating stimulus become increasingly effective; and, on the other hand, *Paramecium's* reactions to a harmless contact stimulus, such as a solid object, decrease in vigour and are soon discontinued.

While the regulative *rôle* played by the physiological state cannot be questioned, certain further inferences of a less warrantable character have at times been deduced from the same data. These inferences assert that the fact of adaptation is evidence of a rudimentary ability to learn by experience, an ability which has frequently been regarded as affording a criterion of the presence of mind. It is implied that *Stentor* in some way 'realises' the inadequacy of its earlier responses or the harmless nature of the stimulus, and modifies its action accordingly. But such an assumption is altogether gratuitous. It is more in accord with the facts to regard these modifications of behaviour as physiologically conditioned. The cessation of response may be compared to the well-known phenomenon of acclimatization to chemicals, a phenomenon adequately explained on a purely chemical basis; while, in the instances where we have a series of increasingly effective responses—each of which, it should be remarked, is more vigorous than the preceding— the phenomenon may be well explained as the outcome of a heightened irritability due in part to the persistence of the stimulus, in part to the preceding avoiding reactions themselves.

The question whether protozoan behaviour presents any features clearly indicating ability to form a habit, as distinct from mere physiological adaptation, must now be considered.

The data at our command are scanty, but some
evidence has been educed to show that *Paramecium* can apparently acquire one habit. The
conditions were as follows :—A *Paramecium* was
placed in a fine glass tube, the diameter of which
was rather less than the animal's length, and
which contained only a very small amount
of water. Owing to the narrowness of the
tube the *Paramecium* had considerable difficulty
in reversing its course therein, having, perforce,
to double on itself in order to turn. The kymo-
graphic records show that within a very few
minutes a number of these creatures came,
in requirement with the conditions, to modify
their usual avoiding reaction by means of pro-
longing the lateral turn. Further, the experimenters, Day and Bentley, found that when
after an interval of from ten to twenty minutes
the same *Paramecia* were again placed in
the capillary-tubes their behaviour contrasted
in two respects with that displayed on the
original trials : (1) the first turns of the second
series were accomplished on the whole more
quickly than those of the first series ; and
(2) the maximum speed and facility of turning
were reached much sooner in the later tests.
These results reveal a certain persistence of

the acquired reaction that immediately suggests analogy with learning by experience. An attempt to interpret the facts as an example of individual learning, however, has met with severe criticism. It is pointed out that the seeming habit may be otherwise accounted for. As is well known, *Paramecium* takes in and excretes water with the most astonishing rapidity. Furthermore, abnormal conditions tend to bring about marked changes in this infusorian's body. It is, therefore, highly probable that, owing to confinement in a small amount of water, such alterations in form, size or consistency as would readily explain the increased facility in turning, may have occurred in this organism; while the second feature, the persistence of the habit after several minutes, is attributable to the partial persistence of the changed physical condition.

There is, therefore, no *clear* proof of the occurrence of any phenomenon requiring for its explanation the presence of consciousness in the Protozoa. Nor is there any evidence to show that these simple creatures are able to profit by experience in any but the most transitory manner. Such modifications as do occur are, indeed, adequately accounted for by a change in physiological condition

brought about by immediately preceding stimulation.

The so-called ' indeterminateness ' frequently
manifested in the behaviour of these micro-
organisms, the random movements upon which
the theory of trial and error is based, have
sometimes been appealed to as affording evidence
of the presence of that spontaneity which is
regarded as an attribute of mind. But Jennings,
who has devoted the utmost care to the observation of these phenomena, never wearies of
insisting that the apparently random movements
are in truth very definitely determined, in part,
by the organism's structure, in part, by its
present condition which is to a large extent
the outcome of its preceding condition. It
is a mistake to suppose that the trial and error
view in contradistinction to the tropistic view
implies chance : on either theory the most
rigid determinism is involved. There is, however, a fundamental difference between the
two, for Jennings' interpretation alone admits
the assumption of *plasticity*.

Now the importance of plasticity lies in
the fact that it affords a basis for further development, whereas the rigid fixity of tropisms, on
the contrary, absolutely prohibits any enduring

modification. Plasticity only requires that the
facts of selection, adaptation, and varied response to a stimulus be raised by means of
the growth of a finer discrimination to their
highest power, in order to present us with an
organism exhibiting objectively all the features
of a very high degree of intelligence—an organism
that would discover the most adequate response
to a stimulus and, modifying its behaviour
accordingly, would retain and make use on
future occasions of the lesson learnt in a single
experience. Such a stage might conceivably
be reached by advancing on the lines laid down
in the trial and error reaction. One of the
chief objections to the tropistic interpretation,
as we have said, is that it precludes any such
advance. Nevertheless, though the available
evidence does not support a tropistic interpretation of the behaviour of the Protozoa, it is by
no means necessary to refuse it a subordinate
place as presenting a more or less true account
of certain phenomena when regarded in isolation.
There is reason to believe, for instance, that
the tropistic hypothesis is the more adequate
to account for the behaviour of these micro-
organisms when subjected to the abnormal
stimulus of a galvanic current.

To sum up, though the activities of uni-
cellular organisms reveal no irrefragable proof
of the presence of mind, a study of their conduct
suffices to exhibit at least a partial resemblance
to so-called 'intelligent' behaviour.

CHAPTER II

If an animal is to make any real progress the effects of experience must be, in some measure, retained Two kinds of retentiveness may be distinguished ; the one, purely physiological ; the other involving consciousness and hence termed psychological. Moreover, conduct that exhibits physiological retentiveness need not involve retentiveness of the psychological, or conscious, kind. For example, among quite lowly animals we find apparent manifestations of conscious retentiveness ; but it behoves us to be wary, since such appearances frequently turn out on further analysis to be illusory, their ascription to memory being possible only through faulty analysis. A case in point is the behaviour of certain Ophiuroids or Brittle-stars. These animals when pulled away from an object will usually, if given the opportunity, return direct to it or, in the event of its removal, to the place it had occupied. Such conduct would seem to imply the retention, somehow, in consciousness of an impression of the object or of its direction. In the light of subsequent observation, however, this assumption appears unnecessary, for it has been found that Ophiuroids tend, in the absence of interfering stimuli, to keep definitely in a direction once adopted, the same ray remaining leader throughout. The whole occurrence probably depends on the persistence of the physiological state originally determining the leading ray (and in consequence the direction); while the heightened irritability of this ray will reinforce the said state.

Another good instance is to be found in the habits of certain Actinians. These animals are found living on the under side as well as on the upper surface of rocks. In the former situation the disc is directed downwards, in the latter upwards. When several individuals selected from both positions were placed in an aquarium between an upper and a lower plate of glass, it was found that either set of animals took up a position corresponding to that occupied on the rocks; but that this tendency appeared to be lost in from one to two days if the animals were prevented from

resuming their accustomed position in the
meantime. In cases such as these we must look
to the inner state of the organism to afford us
a clue of the situation. It is not that the animals
'remember' their previous orientation, but that
any other orientation would be incongruent
with their physiological state, which has become
modified in a certain manner.

The persistence of rhythmical behaviour
for a longer or shorter period, in the absence
of the conditions originally inducing it, presents
another most striking phenomenon. The periodic
migrations of the small green marine worm,
Convoluta roscoffensis, so admirably described
by Dr Keeble in his little book *Plant Animals*
(Cambridge 1910), constitute perhaps the most
interesting example. But for an instance of
a similar phenomenon occurring in a better-
known animal we may turn to the hermit-
crab. The conduct of this decapod has been
found to vary according to the tide; the animal
at low tide persistently avoiding the light
that it constantly seeks at high tide. And this
regular alternation of behaviour has been observed
to persist for three weeks after the crustaceans
had been removed from the influence of the
tides and placed in an aquarium. These and

similar facts may be best explained by supposing
the organism in question to have become through
long wont attuned to the regular alternation of
certain physiological states resulting in different
behaviour. It must further be assumed that,
owing to the latent inertia displayed by organisms,
this attunement once induced is not subject
to sudden alteration but can only gradually
be abolished. If this view be true it is to be
expected that rhythmical habits of long duration
would, in time, come to acquire a certain *quasi*-
independence and continue to persist for a
brief period even in the absence of effective
stimuli. In short, the animal only behaves
in its accustomed manner because it cannot
at once adapt itself to new conditions. The
case is not one of conscious memory but merely
of physiological inertia.

Retentiveness manifests itself under three,
widely different, forms. The first of these, which
we may designate *repetition*, consists in ability to
repeat an action or series of actions once learnt,
and is predominantly motor in character; it is
fundamental in habit-formation, and is based
chiefly on retentiveness of the physiological
order. Contrasted with this are the other two
forms—recognition and recollection—in both of

which retentiveness of the conscious order is supreme. Of *recognition*, it may be said that it involves, primarily, retention of meaning as opposed to repetition of movements. The third form, typified by *recollection*, is only met with at the ideational level. At this stage the past is not only known in so far as it modifies some present percept, but previous experiences may be said, in a sense, to have gained an entity of their own; the subject is able to 'recall' or 'reconstruct' them. In man, recognition frequently though not necessarily starts a train of recollection, but the two must not therefore be confused: since in recognition, as here understood, there is no explicit conscious reference whatsoever to the absent or the past as such; localisation in time being classed, for the purpose of the present essay, under recollection. If this usage of the term is not strictly orthodox it is at least convenient.

Confining our attention for the present to repetition and recognition, it may be noted in passing that the former approximates closely to the purely mechanical; and tends, once started, to carry itself out. The point of real interest, however, is the intimate connexion of the two. Their relation is shown by the fact that repetition

as instanced in a motor habit, for example,
frequently depends for its cue on recognition;
a certain mode of response comes to be associated
with a particular stimulus or object. Conversely,
in the case of animals the only sign of the
presence of recognition is often this very habit
of differential response. For instance, a cat may
be taught to come into a room to be fed when
a certain note is sounded, but will remain where it
is when any other note is struck. We have here
the formation of an artificial habit (coming into
the room to be fed) which is set into operation
by recognition of a particular situation (a certain
auditory experience); and when such habit is
confined to the appropriate stimulus it affords
evidence of the recognition of the significant
note. The remainder of this chapter will be
devoted chiefly to the discussion of motor habits
and their formation, the consideration of recognition as determined by associative memory
being postponed to the succeeding chapter.

The degree of rapidity with which new
motor habits are acquired, together with the
complexity of such habits, affords an index
of a subject's plasticity. And, further, the
more rapidly such habits are acquired and the
greater the length of time they persist after

relatively few experiences, the smaller the probability that we are dealing with purely physiological retentiveness.

Since it is to be expected that, *ceteris paribus*,
habits will be most readily acquired when
connected with the more imperative needs of
the organism, the motives most extensively
employed as incentives to habit-formation are
those of attaining food or shelter. An experiment made on the small fish, *Gobius*, whose
home is a shell, will serve as an example. The
fish was placed in one compartment of a tank
divided into two by a glass screen, its shell
being placed in the other compartment. The
only passage from the one compartment to
the other was by means of a small opening
situated right at one end of the screen. *Gobius*
sought to reach the shell, and in the attempt
collided frequently with the partition. At
length the opening was found and *Gobius* passed
through. Each time the test was repeated
the opening was found with greater precision
and after fewer blunders, until, on the fifth
trial, the fish swam direct to the aperture and
thence straightforward to its home. This case,
which is typical of many others, shows the
learning of a path involving the inhibition

of movements which falsely appear to lead direct to the desired object. Notice, the needful *détour* is not registered at once but is learnt only gradually, a feature distinctive of physiological retentiveness and hence of repetition rather than of recognition.

The fact that animals, when offered sufficient inducement in the shape of food or shelter, can be taught to learn a path, has been utilized as a method of experiment by students of animal behaviour; and from small beginnings this method has been systematically developed and adapted to the needs of various animals, until in the case of birds and rodents the most elaborate mazes, such as that at Hampton Court, have been successfully employed. Indeed, the group of experiments resting on this basis forms, so far, one of the most noticeable features of the work on animal behaviour during the present century.

The essence of the labyrinth method consists in training an animal to select from among various paths and to follow that which alone leads direct to the goal. An incentive suited to the nature of the subjects is usually offered; *e.g.* in the case of monkeys, fruits or nuts; in the case of turtles, the regaining of the nest

or of companionship; and in the case of frogs
water placed at the far end of the labyrinth, etc.
Above all it is important that in each case the
labyrinth employed shall be adapted to the species
tested. Thus for the crayfish a very simple type
of labyrinth is used involving only a single choice
of paths (fig. 4). The apparatus employed

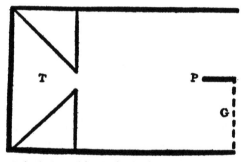

Fig. 4. Labyrinth used by Yerkes and Huggins in experiments on
the crayfish. *T*, compartment from which animal was started;
P, partition at exit; *G*, glass plate closing one exit. (Reproduced from Washburn's *The Animal Mind*, p. 220.)

consists of a box leading to an aquarium.
At the entrance end, two triangular blocks
affixed to either corner insure the subject's
starting out from a central (*i.e.* an indifferent)
position. At the opposite end, adjoining the
aquarium, a longitudinal partition placed mid-
way between the two sides divides the tank at

its upper end into two passages. Either passage can be closed by a glass screen, thereby leaving an open path on one side of the box only. The arrangement will be clear from the figure given above.

At first the correct passage was only selected in 50 per cent. of the trials. But this percentage was gradually raised until with the sixtieth trial it had reached 90 per cent. One individual which underwent a larger number of tests succeeded in forming a 'perfect' habit in 250 trials; and, further, proved able, when the accustomed passage was closed by the screen, to form the new habit of taking the path it had previously learnt to avoid.

As contrasting with this simple type of labyrinth we find at the other end of the scale the use of the Hampton Court maze (fig. 5). This is a highly complex maze in which the true path is very devious and irregular, and necessitates the passing of the entrances to no fewer than six *culs-de-sac*. It has been found to present considerable difficulty even to human beings. Nevertheless it has been successfully learnt by white rats, by an English sparrow, by squirrels, and by monkeys, thus demonstrating the ability of these animals to form a motor habit of considerable complexity.

Moreover the labyrinth habit is a true habit, not to be explained simply by the persistence of a stimulus or by physiological inertia. It has, indeed, been found that many of the animals

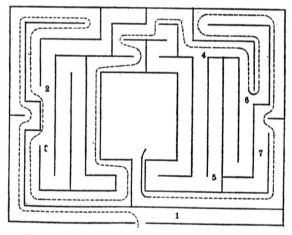

Fig. 5.   Hampton Court Maze.   (After Kinnaman.)

tested show even after relatively long periods almost perfect memory of the particular habit acquired. Also, in cases where a habit is not perfectly retained over an interval, it is, nevertheless, generally true that the habit is relearnt with fewer trials than were originally required, thus proving the presence of a certain degree of retention. In the case of the pigeon a simple labyrinth habit was still practically perfect at the end of four weeks, although no further training had been given in the meantime. A cowbird, which proved relatively slow in learning a maze, when tested after an interval of thirty days, completely recovered the habit by the fourth test. Guinea-pigs were found to retain perfect familiarity with a labyrinth path at the end of forty-eight days. A female monkey, also, gave distinct evidence of retention of the Hampton Court maze after a period of one hundred days had elapsed from the learning tests; during which time she had been re-tested only once and that on the fiftieth day. Even the crayfish, whose behaviour was described above, made 70 per cent. of right choices after an interval of two weeks.

Since the ability of various animals to learn and retain labyrinth paths of various complexity has been clearly demonstrated, it is desirable to proceed further and to discover the nature of the processes that enter into the formation of the habit. Here the white rat will best serve as an example, its behaviour in this connexion having been subjected to more careful analysis than, perhaps, that of any other animal. How then, we may inquire, does this rodent learn a path through a maze ? Which of the various receptors (or sense-organs) are called into play ?

That vision is not absolutely essential is shown by the numerous experiments proving the white rat's ability to learn a maze in the dark, or when deprived of the use of its eyes. Also, rats whose ears have been filled with paraffin-wax, rats in which the olfactory nerves have been rendered insensitive, and rats with the vibrissae cut, have all learnt mazes—facts which prove that auditory impressions, olfactory impressions and tactile impressions received through the vibrissae are none of them indispensable. One rat even when deprived simultaneously of impressions received through the visual, tactile, and olfactory end-organs succeeded in learning a labyrinth. From these and kindred observations Watson was led to deduce that the white rat's success in learning a maze is dependent chiefly on its kinaesthetic and organic 'sensations,' i.e. on sensations arising from muscular and visceral activity.

More recent experiments, however, suggest that the importance of the tactile sense has hitherto been underestimated. For it was noticed that when rats with the head and nose vibrissae clipped are set to learn a maze, they frequently bump their heads or noses at the corners against the walls. The records reveal a definite correlation between the number of these corner-contacts and the number of errors, the contacts gradually decreasing as the habit comes to be acquired, but increasing again the instant hesitation or uncertainty occurs. Hence it may be assumed that the contact sense normally plays some part in the rat's learning of a laby-rinth. Whether the senses of sight, smell, etc., play a subsidiary *rôle* remains uncertain, but it is not disproved by the fact that they have been shown not to be indispensable.

It has just been remarked that the number of head-contacts decrease and finally vanish completely as the habit becomes perfect; from which it appears that factors involved in the learning of a habit may be entirely unnecessary to the successful performance of the habit when learnt. Therefore whilst admitting that the contact-sense is of the utmost importance during the actual learning, it is not inconsistent to assert that the rat's running of a labyrinth when learnt is controlled almost entirely by kinaesthetic and organic cues. That such is

indeed the case there is abundant evidence
to prove. For example, if, after rats have learnt
a maze, a portion of it be removed, whereby
certain of the runways are shortened while the
general relations of the maze are left intact, it
will be found that the animals at first invariably
bump into the end-walls of the reduced alleys.
On the other hand, when it is the shortened
form of maze that is first learnt, it will be found
that the rats, on being tested subsequently
in the lengthened maze, will constantly attempt
to round the alleys at the former accustomed
distances, regardless of the absence of openings.
In either case vision is inoperative. It is of
interest to note that this would seem not to
hold true of the pigeon. For on being given
similar tests this bird was never observed to
butt into the walls.

The above facts suggest that the running
of a labyrinth path becomes, in time, an automatic habit requiring the minimum of attention
for its performance. In this as in other respects
it closely resembles the playing of memorized
music. Just as in the playing of a familiar
melody each movement of the fingers prompts
the next position of the hand, so each movement
of a trained rat running the maze inevitably

suggests the succeeding movement. The tendency displayed by rats (as also by squirrels and turtles) to return to the starting point on any slip, error, hesitation or interruption, no matter how near the goal they may be, and to make an entirely fresh beginning, rather than to take up the path from the point where they were interrupted or to correct themselves *en route*, bears out the analogy. For likewise upon interruption the pianist who has learnt his piece must generally make a completely new start, or at least return to the beginning of a phrase.

This automaticity, characterising the acquired maze habit, is rendered possible by the gradual transference, during learning, of the control from cues derived through the extero-ceptors (*i.e.* the end-organs which receive impressions derived from the external world) to cues derived through the proprio-ceptors (*i.e.* the end-organs whose stimuli are the changes going on in the deep tissues of the organism, *e.g.* in the muscles, tendons, and blood-vessels). The rat, as we have seen, relies at first chiefly on contact cues, possibly also on visual and olfactory cues; but these in time give place to kinaesthetic and organic

cues which ultimately assume complete dominance. From the intimate relationship shown
to exist between kinaesthesis and automatism,
it will be readily understood that on the introduction of the slightest change in the conditions
of the maze the subjects once more fall back
on the extero-ceptors; the proprio-ceptors, on
account of the readiness with which they lend
themselves to the automatizing of behaviour,
being ill-adapted to cope with situations requiring
rapid readjustment.

Not only may there be this transference
from extero-ceptive to proprio-ceptive, but Hunter
has further succeeded in proving that under
certain conditions one set of cues may come
to be replaced by another set, derived through
the same extero-ceptor as the first. His subjects
were pigeons. After a maze had been learnt
by the birds it was rotated first through 90°
and later through 270°. Birds that were considerably confused by the first rotation made
perfect records on the further rotation. Hunter's
observations strongly suggest that whereas the
birds had at first in great part relied on visual
cues afforded by objects outside the maze,
they later came, on the failure of these, to adopt
in their stead certain visual features presented

by the interior of the maze. Unlike the white rat, the pigeon, it will be remembered, is always to some extent dependent on vision in running the maze, the labyrinth habit, therefore, never acquiring such a high degree of automatism in its case as in the case of the rat.

Yet another feature must be mentioned as the outcome of the automaticity characteristic of the perfected labyrinth habit. It is now ascertained (judging by objective data) that rats do not learn mazes with markedly greater facility after having had experience in previous mazes. But since the increased acquaintance with the general nature of labyrinths, and the growing association with the reward received at the end, must count as advantageous, the relatively slight degree of transfer whether positive or negative can only be attributed to the automatizing nature of the process. For automatism, as has already been pointed out, makes against adaptation or innovation within its own sphere of authority. While it renders the subject in some respects more independent of its environment, for that very reason it throws him off his guard and leaves him less prepared to meet any novel situation which may arise. This comes out very clearly in the behaviour of the white rat with its tendency to make stereotyped turns at certain definite distances, regardless of whether they are appropriate to the conditions prevailing at the moment.

Speaking generally of the relative difficulties presented by the various features of a maze, it may be said that as a rule rats experience greater difficulty in learning to avoid *culs-de-sac* than in mastering a new turn or a short cut. And when a familiar labyrinth path is modified, the new turn is more easily learnt the nearer it is to the entrance; indeed, it would seem that in such modifications of route a long familiar final portion constitutes an essential to ready acquisition.

While dealing with the labyrinth method, it should be insisted that the ability of animals to learn quickly and to traverse without error labyrinths of varying complexity by no means constitutes (as might at first be mistakenly supposed) an index of their ' general intelligence.' At most it affords a criterion of their ability to form a certain type of motor habit. For example, on comparing the results yielded by the different classes of subjects tested by this method, it is found that rodents, especially white rats, far excel all the other species; birds and monkeys proving considerably inferior, while the records of human subjects show little if any superiority. It is clear, therefore, that the maze habit is one requiring either a minimum of intelligence or intelligence of a very specific and limited kind: and herein lies its great value, for it provides an experiment, which is almost a pure test of plasticity, and in which general intelligence plays a very slight part.

In conclusion, a word must be said about the various methods used to determine the rate of formation of a labyrinth habit. Three different kinds of records have been employed. They consist in noting respectively (*a*) the *time* required for each run from start to finish; (*b*) the complete *distance*, including all returns on the true path and entries into *culs-de-sac*, traversed by the animal during the run; (*c*) the number of *errors* made on each trial. Of these three methods the error record, for which no conventional standard has as yet been agreed upon, is the most variable. Experimenters differ as to the evaluation of the various types of errors. For instance, are all errors, whatever their nature, to be accounted of equal value? Should returns upon the true path be classed with entries into blind alleys? Is not immediate withdrawal upon entering a *cul-de-sac* to be distinguished from the traversing of its entire length? And are partial returns upon the true path to be equated with total returns ? Either the errors must be quantitatively estimated, in which case the error method becomes nothing more than a rough application of the distance method ; or the errors must be qualitatively distinguished. In this latter event, however, it is evident that the method requires careful standardisation before it can be adopted for comparative purposes. The time record, on the other hand, has been objected to on the ground that it covers apparently irrelevant behaviour, such as pauses, the stopping of animals *en route* to perform their toilet, loitering, etc. ; nevertheless, for comparative work, it proves the most satisfactory record of the three and is the only one which takes into account all the phases of the process of learning. The distance record presents far more difficulties as regards practical procedure than either of the other two, and is, as well, very much more laborious. An elaborate analysis of the three systems indicates that a combination of the time and error records for the various trials is, on the whole, the most representative and practical method for comparative purposes.

With regard to the signification of these various methods of record, it is of interest to note that comparative work on rats and human adult subjects has shown (*a*) that whereas rats decrease their time records on successive trials relatively faster than their errors, the reverse holds true of human subjects ; (*b*) that whereas the time taken by rats to run a maze decreases sevenfold as compared with the distance, it is only relatively slightly decreased by human adults ; and lastly (*c*) that whereas human adults at first decrease the distance rapidly as compared with the errors, rats, on the other hand, show little difference in these records during the earlier tests, the relatively greater decrease in distance only occurring in the later tests. This last, it has been thought, may afford some sort of criterion as to the order of intelligent ability, if any, manifested. For while a glance into a wrong alley suffices, even at an early period, to assure the human subject of his error, the rat at a similar stage continues right on to the end of the *cul-de-sac* before discovering its mistake. Experience in running different mazes, however, brings the rat's behaviour more into line with that of human subjects according to Wiltbank.

The evidence afforded by the use of the labyrinth method at least proves that various animals, from the crayfish to man, may be taught to modify their behaviour in response to the requirements of the environment, and to retain such modification over relatively long periods. The process presents another aspect, however, in that the acquirement of such modification in the form of a habit appears to render the establishment of subsequent modifications of a similar character more difficult in certain respects.

CHAPTER III

It is a fact of common knowledge that objects or occurrences, in themselves indifferent or unmeaning, may come to derive secondary interest or meaning through association with events possessed of intrinsic significance for the subject. Everyone knows the excited interest displayed by the house cat or dog upon hearing the dinner gong. The behaviour displayed is quite characteristic and is not to be called forth by the ringing of the telephone bell or by the chiming of a clock. In other words the sound of the gong has meaning; it is recognised. Through previous experience it has become a sign of the feast that is to follow.

Now it is just this very fact of meaning being acquired through individual experience which constitutes the cardinal point of recognition. Whence it follows that all cases not

requiring individual experience for their explanation must be excluded from our rubric. Nevertheless, despite our canon, the line of cleavage
is not absolutely sharp, certain border-line
cases occurring in which, at present, definite
decision is impossible. The behaviour of the
tube-worm, *Hydroides dianthus*, may serve as
an example. *H. dianthus* reacts almost invariably to mechanical stimulation (*e.g.* the
touch of a glass rod) by withdrawing into its
tube. A sudden decrease in the intensity of
the light (as produced by dropping a black card-
board screen between the window and the dish
containing the worms) may likewise occasion a
similar effect. But the response to shadows is
not nearly so constant as that to a mechanical
stimulus; some individuals, indeed, cease to
respond as early as the third shadow when
the succession is fairly rapid. The experiment
consisted in combining both forms of stimulation,
the casting of each shadow being followed immediately by a touch from the glass rod.
Upon subsequently testing the animals with
shadows alone, it was found that the shrinking
reaction was elicited far more constantly than
had been the case prior to training. Now a
possible explanation of the increased frequency

of response to the photic stimulus may, of course, be found in the heightened irritability consequent upon repeated mechanical stimulation. But some doubt as to the adequacy of such explanation arises in view of the relatively high degree of persistency of the modification, a regular and marked increase in the number of reactions to shadows continuing, in one case, for seven days.

A less disputable instance is afforded by Cowles's observations on the small crab, *Ocypoda*. These crustaceans, though land-dwellers, require to keep their gills constantly moistened; and to this end a dish containing water was placed in their enclosure. Cowles noticed that in a very few days contact with the empty glass would alone suffice to call forth the characteristic drinking response. The fact that individual experience here played a part seems unquestionable.

Mainly because it presents in general such a clear manifestation of individually acquired modification or of learning through experience, many writers have come to see in this phenomenon of associative memory a touchstone of mind. Very little reflexion, however, will serve to show that before this criterion can be adopted *ad hoc*, it requires considerable amplification and refining. As various workers have already pointed out, the rapidity with which associations are formed, together with their complexity and relative permanence when formed, must be taken into account. Are we to consider, for example, that a turtle requiring 290 trials before coming to discriminate between two sets of 8 mm. lines, similar in all respects save that the one set is vertical, the other horizontal, affords by its ultimate success an indubitable proof of consciousness ?

But the phenomenon of associative memory has been used in other ways than as criterion of mind; and it is to these that we must now turn our attention.

First then, if used judiciously, we have in the principle of associative memory a means of testing the degree of strength of any instinct or habit; and, where any such instinct can be broken down, through the means of the same principle, we have proof that it is not tropistic in character. Take the case of the May-fly nymph, *Heptagenia interpunctata*. This insect is said to be negatively phototactic (*i.e.* always to head away from the direction of light rays). If, however, its negative phototaxis is pitted against another deep-seated tendency, namely that of seeking and clinging to a stone—sometimes known as ' thigmotaxis '—so that in order to reach the stone the nymph is forced to travel directly towards the source of light, it is found that after some weeks' training the distance from which the insect will approach the stone is much greater than at first ; a fact affording evidence that its negative phototaxis has been thus far overcome.

Perhaps the most striking example of the inhibition of instinctive reaction, yet produced by this method, is to be found in Triplett's experiments on the perch. Two perch were placed in one compartment of an aquarium and several minnows in the other, the smaller fish being separated from the larger by a glass screen. The perch at first continually tried to reach the minnows, butting their heads frequently against the screen in the attempt ; but, at the end of a month, while still watching the minnows, they had learnt to avoid contact with the screen. The completeness of the inhibition is shown by the fact that when a minnow was placed in the same compartment with the perch, the larger fish confined themselves at first to watching it, following, however,

when it made a rapid dart ; though eventually
even the impulse to dart was inhibited. Nevertheless, when the minnows were replaced by
worms dangled in the farther compartment,
the perch once more collided with the screen
in their attempts to reach the new delicacy,
thereby clearly demonstrating the specialised
nature of the inhibition.

Another and more extensive use to which
the principle of associative memory has been
put, is the testing of sensory discrimination.
In this connexion it may serve two rather
different purposes :

(i) It may be employed to demonstrate
an animal's ability to perceive a particular
class of stimuli, *e.g.* photic, acoustic, etc., which
normally produce no appreciable effect. Thus
for a long time it was thought that fishes were
devoid of hearing, since no sounds other than
those resulting in concussion (*e.g.* blasting) or
in an actual shaking of the aquarium (*e.g.* a
tap on the side of the tank)—which could
therefore be adequately accounted for by dermal
sensations—produced any appreciable effect or
elicited any response. The classical exception of
the monastery fishes that were supposed to
come for food on the ringing of a bell was

long ago shown by Kreidl to be really a visual response; for the fish would assemble in similar manner at the sight of a person even though the bell was not rung, whereas the approach of any one remaining unseen, even though they rang the bell, had no effect whatsoever. Parker, however, by carefully designed tests has been able to demonstrate that the fish, *Fundulus heteroclitus*, does respond to sound-waves which are certainly received through the ear. His apparatus consisted of a tank, one end of which was made of wood and served as a sounding-board. From the middle of one of the vertical edges of the latter a wooden arm projected horizontally outward. At the free-end of this arm a bass-viol string was stretched to the opposite end of the sounding-board; this when plucked gave 40 vibrations per second. Later this stimulus was replaced by an electric tuning-fork (128 vibrations per second) which was so arranged that when sounded it did not produce any vibratory movement of the aquarium as a whole, nor even any ripple. The fish under experimentation was placed in a small cage suspended in the tank, its support being, however, entirely independent of the walls of the aquarium. One of the sides of the cage was

made of wire-netting and this side directly
faced the source of the sound.   Three groups
of subjects were employed : (A) normal fishes,
(B) fishes whose auditory nerves had been
severed or whose ear-organs had been completely
removed, (C) fishes in which the general integu-
ment had been rendered insensitive but in
which the ears were intact.   The experimenter's
movements were executed out of sight of the
fish, and after they had come to rest at the
bottom of the cage.   The results obtained
showed that the normal *Fundulus* gave well-
defined responses, consisting chiefly of movements
of the pectoral fins and an increase in the rate
of respiration, to the stimuli in question.   The
fish of group B, on the other hand, did not respond to the sound-waves from the tuning-fork ;
whereas the fishes whose skin had been rendered
insensitive gave reactions that were surprisingly
clear and decisive, exhibiting, as far as the
vibrating chord was concerned, the essential
characteristics of normal individuals.   Various
considerations point to the fact that the failure
of the earless fish to respond to the given stimuli
was indeed ' due to the loss of the ear as a sense-
organ and not to secondary complications ac-
companying the operation.'   The reaction-times

together with control experiments further demonstrated that the A and C groups did respond to true sound-waves (*i.e.* waves received through the ear) as opposed to the movement of the aquarium as a whole or to the wave movement indicated by ripples. These facts taken together clearly prove that *Fundulus*, at least, is able to perceive auditory stimuli.

(ii) The principle of associative memory may be employed not only to prove the perception of a certain class of stimuli, but also to determine the nature and delicacy of such perception. To this end it has been used with all the main types of stimuli, but most extensively with those of a visual character. By its means, in the sphere of vision, the discrimination of brightness, hue, size and form by many species of animals has been successfully investigated. The method pursued consists essentially in the combining of an originally indifferent stimulus, auditory or visual, etc., as the case may be, with something possessing inherent interest for the animal, such as food, home, or even punishment. Two or more degrees or qualities of the stimulus tested (the reward or absence of punishment being associated for the time being only with one of these) are presented repeatedly to the

subject until such time as proof is obtained
of his ability (or inability) to distinguish between
them under the conditions of the test. Consistently reacting in an appropriate manner
to the opposed stimuli constitutes the proof.
If success is achieved, the difference between
the stimuli may be reduced, and discrimination
once more tested under the new conditions.
The reduction of the difference between the two
stimuli may be continued until a point is reached
where the subject, despite prolonged training, is
no longer able to distinguish between them.
The procedure may perhaps be more readily understood if one or two concrete examples are given.

Starting with the simplest case, that of the
investigation of *brightness discrimination*, this
procedure cannot be better exemplified than by
Yerkes' now classical observations on the dancing
mouse. In the final form of his experiments
Yerkes' apparatus consisted of a nest-box, opening, by means of a swinging door, into a second
compartment, the entrance chamber (see fig. 6).
At the opposite end of this second chamber
were two square apertures, each of which formed
the entrance to a box (the discrimination or
electric-box) communicating with an alley that
led back to the home-box; either alley could

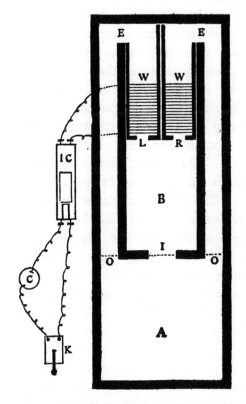

Fig. 6. Ground plan of discrimination-box. *A*, nest-box; *B*, entrance chamber; *W*, *W*, electric-boxes; *L*, doorway of left electric-box; *R*, doorway of right electric-box; *E*, exit from electric-box to alley; *I*, swinging door between *A* and *B*; *O*, swinging door between alley and *A*; *IC*, induction apparatus; *C*, electric cell; *K*, key in circuit. (After Yerkes.)

be blocked at will. The floor in both dis-
crimination-boxes consisted of an oak board
carrying electric wires that were connected up
with an induction apparatus. The general
arrangement was such that the shock could
be given in either box, as desired, provided
that the circuit was completed by the dancer's
feet being in contact with two of the wires,
on the floor of the box. Each discrimination-
box was ' illuminated independently by the
light from incandescent lamps directly above
them....The light-box [containing the lamps]
was pivoted [so that it] could be turned through
an angle of 180° by the experimenter.' The
lamps could be moved up or down and the
brightness of the electric-boxes thereby regulated;
the distance being indicated on a scale. In
general the height of one lamp only (the variable)
was altered during a series, the position of the
other (the standard) remaining constant. In
one experiment 20 hefner units of light intensity
were taken as the standard. A mouse choosing
the compartment which displayed this degree
of illumination found a clear passage direct
to the nest : whereas entrance into the other
compartment was punished by an electric shock,
coupled with the fact that the nest could only

be regained by an indirect route. In order
to insure against the risk of mistaking a mere
position habit (such as that of going always to
the right or to the left-hand box) for brightness
discrimination, the position of the standard
and the variable light was reversed, by means
of the pivot arrangement previously referred
to, the order followed being irregular; but
care was taken that in any series each box
should be illuminated the same number of times
by standard as by variable. Yerkes considered
' 25 wrong choices per hundred as indicative
of a just perceivable difference in illumination.'
Using this criterion of discrimination, it was
found that the dancer could just distinguish
a standard light of 20 hefners from another
light when the difference between them was
approximately $\frac{1}{2}$; while with a standard of
80 hefners a difference of $\frac{1}{5}$th, and with a standard
of 5 hefners a difference of $\frac{1}{10}$th, sufficed. Such
results are highly anomalous, since we should
expect to find Weber's law—that within the
same modality the same ratio holds between
any pair of just discriminable stimuli—conformed
to within the range employed. In order to make
quite sure that the case really did constitute
an exception, each standard was tested afresh.

But this time different results were obtained, the same difference, namely $\frac{1}{10}$th, being found to exist between the just discriminable variable and the standard for all three values of the latter : the case is therefore according to rule. Yet as it was just possible that this relation also might prove to be only a transitory phase, opportunity was given for the mice to learn to discriminate between the original standards and new variables differing from them by only $\frac{1}{15}$th ; in no case, however, even after considerable training was any discrimination shown. This negative evidence in conjunction with the former positive results makes it seem highly probable that Weber's law holds true, after all, for the brightness discrimination of the dancer. The surprising results at first obtained may be satisfactorily explained by the difference of practice in the three cases.

The same procedure, *mutatis mutandis*, has been successfully extended to the investigation of thermal sensibility in the grey squirrel and white rat.

The observations on brightness discrimination in a vast variety of animals are legion, but in only comparatively few cases as yet, has the refined technique of Yerkes' method been employed; at the other end of the scale a much more rough and ready method passes muster. The only apparatus required by this latter method is two or more vessels covered by grey papers of different brightness, food being placed always, during the same series, in vessels covered by one particular shade of grey. The same plan, it will be observed, is common to both methods, but the technique has undergone considerable evolution in the former instance. The inferiority of the more naïve method is immediately obvious from the number and nature of the objections to which it is open. A few of the more glaring of these are the possibility of differences in the texture of the paper, or of its surface when pasted on the vessels giving rise to discrimination apart from true brightness discrimination; another possible source of confusion may arise from the subjects coming to base their judgments on difference in smell, paper being so readily impregnated by odours. But the most fundamental criticism to be urged is that of the hopeless inexactitude of the use of reflected light, and the impossibility of obtaining papers of a pure grey free from any admixture of hue, difficulties which can only be overcome by the use of transmitted light.

The investigation of *colour vision* in animals has been carried out on closely similar lines. But unfortunately the greater number of observations so far made are valueless as regards their bearing on the problem in hand, colour. And they fail by reason of their omission to ascertain, even approximately, the brightness value *for the subject*, of the colours employed   It is true that in many experiments great pains have been taken to match every tone used with a grey of the same degree of brightness, such labour, however, is but vain so long as the match is only made for the human eye, for we have no guarantee that similar brightness relations hold in the case of animals. Indeed, there is evidence to show that the contrary is true, in certain instances at least. For example, it seems to be established beyond doubt that in daylight red appears very much darker to the dancing mouse than it does to the normal human eye; though Waugh found, on the other hand, that albino mice do not show any discrimination between white and red lights. Other recent observations suggest that blue possesses an extremely high brightness value for the rabbit as also for the chick. It is tempting to compare such facts with the brightness

value of the spectrum for the dark-adapted
human eye. Our present concern with them,
however, is simply to bring to notice the manner
in which the investigation of colour discrimination is complicated by the intimate relationship
existing between colour and brightness. As to
the outcome of the small body of observations
which have complied with the more rigorous
conditions involved by this relationship, one
fact clearly emerges, and that is, that colour
plays on the whole a relatively unimportant
rôle in the life of the higher animals. Generally
speaking, however, it may be said that the
interest of these experiments at present lies
rather in the method adopted than in the specific
results obtained. Unfortunately any detailed
account of these researches is impossible in
the limited space at our disposal.

Passing on to the investigation of the visual
discrimination of *form*, it may first be noted
that our subject falls naturally into two sub-
divisions, according as two-dimensional or three-
dimensional objects are employed. Since with
the latter investigation very little headway
has yet been made in the case of animals, our
attention may be confined chiefly to the
former.

The method customarily adopted is one or
another variant of the following general plan.
Two or more cards, of which at least one bears
a device in black on white or the reverse (unless
instead it is cut so as to permit of light passing
through an opening of a certain shape), are displayed either simultaneously or successively.
One of the cards, when rightly understood,
stands as a sign of food or some other reward,
while the other card may denote some punishment such as the shock from an induction coil.
The task before the subject is to learn to react
appropriately to these different signs irrespective
of their relative positions, choosing the food-card
and avoiding the punishment card. Such then
is the method.   Let us now turn to the results.

Beginning with the ordinary English sparrow,
this bird has been taught to distinguish an
unmarked card from a card bearing a black
horizontal bar.   The same bird, as well as
a cow-bird, also learnt to distinguish between
two cards, one of which bore a black diamond,
the other three horizontal lines.   Curiously
enough this same sparrow appeared totally
incapable of discriminating between vessels of
different shape.   Its behaviour, therefore, is the
exact reverse of that of Kinnaman's macaques.

For these latter, while they learnt relatively rapidly to distinguish vessels of different shape, gave no sign whatsoever of any ability to discriminate between cards bearing different devices. Some *Cebus* monkeys observed by Thorndike exhibited, on the other hand, various degrees of proficiency in discriminating cards bearing one dot or three dots, a Y or a Δ, 'YES' or 'N' etc. It is just possible that the slight difference of treatment in the two cases may be partly responsible for the diverse results, Kinnaman displaying both cards simultaneously while Thorndike only presented one card at a time to his subjects. That this is the true explanation is, however, highly improbable; for, in general, the difference works the other way, the method of simultaneous presentation producing, of the two, the better results.

So far, however, not one of the instances described can be regarded as affording conclusive proof of ability to perceive contour or to discriminate form. Each is open to the same objection, namely that the subject may be merely reacting to difference in the mass or extent of the illuminated areas. Later experimenters have profited by the criticism of previous work; and by taking the precaution to insure

that the figures used, while of different patterns,
should yet more or less correspond (an equal
area of illumination being presented in both
cases; fig. 7) they have removed this objection.
Tests which satisfy these more stringent conditions have been given to turtles, dancing mice,
chickens and dogs; the last-mentioned, with

Fig. 7.   Designs used in experiments on Form Discrimination.
(After Casteel.)

one chick, alone giving evidence of form discrimination under these conditions. The same
chicks likewise failed to attain even the sparrow's
standard, proving unable to discriminate two
black cards one of which bore a white triangle
and the other a white square, or two white
cards each of which displayed two black bars

of equal area but differently arranged, one pair being parallel, the other forming an angle. Though another group of chicks when presented with grain cut into squares and triangles, one set of which were gummed down to the food-tray, soon learnt to confine their pecking solely to grains of the other shape. Other factors may well have been responsible for discrimination in this last instance however.

As regards the discrimination of *size*, we may cite the case of the raccoons which came to distinguish a card $4\frac{1}{2}$ in. square from one $6\frac{1}{2}$ in. square, climbing on a box when the larger was shown and remaining motionless when the smaller was exposed. Chicks also readily learnt to discriminate between two similarly shaped apertures of different size (6·35 cm. × 8·89 cm. and 8·89 cm. × 12·44 cm. respectively) opening into passages, one of which led eventually to an exit from the experiment-box. Control series were given to eliminate the influence of brightness.

It will have been remarked that the incentive to learning in the majority of the above experiments consists either of a reward or of a punishment; occasionally of a conjunction of the two, wrong 'choices' being punished, correct 'choices' rewarded. Each system has its adherents; and a long controversy has been,

and still is, waged as to their relative merits.
Briefly stated, the net outcome of the discussion
is to the effect that a method of punishment is
unsatisfactory in so far as it reduces the subjects
to a state of fear or panic, and thus places
them at a disadvantage for acquiring new habits ;
but, that it is superior to a method of reward
in that it insures more constant conditions.
The difficulties of the reward system are (*a*) to
find rewards which are both practicable and at
the same time attractive to the animals ; (*b*)
the fluctuation in attraction which such rewards
invariably undergo, owing to the changes that
take place in an animal's physiological state.
The attractive power of the favourite reward,
food, for example, is well known to vary considerably, and is, at best, of comparatively
short duration unless the animal is in a state
of utter hunger, in which case, however, the
method of reward (food) is open to an objection
similar to that already brought against punishment : namely, that an animal when in a state of
keen hunger is not in the condition best suited
for the exercise of delicate discrimination and
the acquiring of new and strange habits.

    An attempt has been made to determine
in a more exact manner the relative values

of these various systems. The subjects of
the experiment were rats; and the task appointed them, that of discriminating between
two lights of different intensity. The apparatus
employed was similar to that used by Yerkes
in his tests on brightness discrimination (fig. 6).
The animals were divided into three groups,
of which group A was rewarded with food
for right ' choices,' and group B punished
with a slight electric shock for wrong ' choices,'
while group C was punished or rewarded according as the ' choice ' was wrong or right.
The results of the investigation indicate that
in the given conditions a method of combined
punishment and reward is more effective than
is either component when used in isolation,
the rats of group C acquiring the said habit
in the shortest time. As regards the opposed
claims of punishment and reward, the former
must be looked upon as proving the more
potent in the present case, in respect of rate
of learning at least, since the members of group A
alone failed to form the habit in the period
allowed (590 trials).

Nor do we find any greater unanimity when
we pass on to consider the most favourable
degree of shock, since it is impossible to frame

any clear-cut rule on the very slender basis
of the scanty data available. Furthermore,
the failure to detect any such general principle
can scarcely be regarded as surprising, as it is
not at all improbable that the optimal strength
of stimulus varies for different species and even
among the individual members of a group. On
one point, however, two of the existing researches
agree; for, both Yerkes with dancing mice
and Cole with chicks found that where the
conditions of discrimination are relatively easy
the optimal degree of shock is considerably above
the threshold of stimulation. But whereas in
the case of all *successful* chicks the application
of a strong stimulus appeared to be more
effective than a weak one even in cases
where discrimination was difficult, it proved
otherwise with the mouse, for Yerkes states that
'the more difficult the habit the weaker the
stimulus which most quickly forces its acquisition.' Curiously enough Cole obtained a closely
similar result from the chicks which failed to
form the difficult habit; for judging by the
proportion of chicks failing with different degrees
of punishment it appeared that 'the optimal
stimulus recedes...to a point nearer the threshold of stimulation than in the case of medium

discrimination.' The one drawback to Cole's tests is that he failed to give control series without the use of punishment.

This chapter cannot be brought to a close without some mention being made of the salivary reflex method, originated by Pawlow and only later introduced to Western Europe. The method, as its name implies, is based on the reaction of the salivary glands It is a fact of everyday experience that the introduction of food or chemicals into the mouth causes a flow of saliva ; not only so, but at times even the mere sight of food will make ' the mouth water.' There is an important difference, however, between the two cases, for whereas the former instance, in which the stimulus acts directly, constitutes an example of a true, invariable or, to use Pawlow's terminology, ' unconditioned ' reflex, the latter, where the stimulus acts at a distance and which, given the proper conditions, may be abolished, typifies on the other hand a ' conditioned ' reflex.

In order to bring about a ' conditioned ' reflex to a certain stimulus, *e.g.* a given degree of light intensity, the procedure generally adopted is as follows :—An animal, kept in darkness, is subjected repeatedly to the ' food-stimulus,'

light, each exposure being invariably either
accompanied or quickly followed by the presentation of food or the introduction into the mouth
of some chemical that occasions an ' unconditioned ' reflex. In time, if the new reflex forms,
the appearance of the light in itself suffices
to produce the salivary flow. Whereupon the
next step consists in defining the reflex. The
particular degree of light constituting the food-
stimulus may now be replaced at times by
either a much dimmer or a brighter light, un-
accompanied, however, by food. Should these
new degrees of light intensity also cause a flow
of saliva the experimenter continues to alternate
them irregularly with the food-stimulus until
such time as the salivary reflex is confined
to the latter alone, or he decides that it is
useless to carry the experience further, the
particular reflex in all probability not admitting
of more precise definition.

Not only does this method serve to discover
the variety of stimuli with which conditioned
reflexes may be formed—pressure, temperature,
scratch, smell, light, visual movement, sound,
etc., have all been employed with success—
together with their order of importance for the
animal tested ; but it also presents us with

a new means of determining the ability of certain animals to distinguish between stimuli differing either qualitatively or quantitatively. Its superiority over the more usual method of the ' motor reaction ' lies in its reflex character, its more automatic nature, its greater 'involunta-riness' and precision as contrasted with the more or less ' voluntary' character of movements. At the same time this very immediacy of response, together with its independence of intelligence and its freedom from direct volitional control, make it doubtful how far the formation of conditioned reflexes involves actual conscious dis-crimination as distinct from the simple acquire-ment of new neural habits or the establishment of new neural connexions. That it is impossible to form certain conditioned reflexes, *e.g.* reaction to visual form, after the extirpation of a particular region of the visual cortex renders it in some degree probable, however, that in such cases true sensory discrimination may be involved.

Lastly, the salivary reflex method enables us to determine quantitatively, in a manner relatively fine and exact, the laws governing cerebral association—its formation, extinction, revival, etc.

As an illustration of the method, Selionyi's

experiment on auditory reactions in the dog may be briefly summarised.

The operative procedure consisted in exposing the duct of one of the salivary glands, *e.g.* the parotid. Into this opening a small glass funnel was introduced ; this funnel in connexion with a tube conveyed the saliva to a graduated vessel. The amount of secretion, its viscidity and the latent period between the occurrence of the stimulus and the appearance of the first drop of saliva could thus be exactly determined.

The object of the experiments was to determine 'how great must be the difference in the quality or the intensity of two auditory stimuli in order that they shall produce perceivably different effects upon the auditory apparatus of the dog.' The stimuli consisted of sounds from an organ, two whistles, a trumpet, metronomes, etc. Having ascertained that unfamiliar sounds did not normally produce a secretion of saliva, Selionyi proceeded to discover whether, by feeding his subjects whenever a certain note was sounded, a conditioned reflex, *i.e.* a reflex produced by sounding the note in the absence of food, could be brought about. His efforts were successful, from 20 to 40 experiences sufficing. Moreover, the auditory-salivary reflex, when formed, proved to possess a high degree of specificity, the salivary flow being either absent or markedly modified if another note differing slightly in pitch, timbre, intensity or by a quarter tone were substituted for the food-stimulus. With chords too, it was found impossible to replace, add, or suppress a single note. Such reflexes once initiated were found, when not interfered with, to persist for two months.

Selionyi was likewise successful in forming a conditioned reflex to the *cessation* of sound. The metronome was allowed to beat from 5–20 minutes; at the moment it stopped, hydrochloric acid (which, when introduced into the mouth, occasions an unconditioned salivary reflex) was given to the animal. After twenty tests the stoppage of the metronome or even a decrease in its rate, by itself brought about a copious flow of saliva.

The extinction of such conditioned reflexes is easily managed, a few experiences of the accidental stimulus (in this case auditory) dissociated from the essential stimulus (food or drug) sufficing to accomplish this end. But such destruction, it is interesting to observe, is also rigidly specific.

This brief description will, it is hoped, make clear the immense value of the salivary reflex method as furnishing an instrument for determining the different stimuli towards which an animal is capable of learning to react characteristically and consistently. And it can readily be understood what a valuable adjunct Pawlow's method forms to the older methods based on associative memory; for the chief use of these latter lie, as this chapter has tried to show, in the means which they afford of determining the relative paucity or richness of an animal's sensory equipment—a determination which must be made prior to any extensive consideration of its higher ' mental ' processes.

CHAPTER IV

INSTINCT

In the preceding chapter mention was made of the fact that under certain conditions the instinctive response normally elicited by certain objects may come to be modified as the result of individual experience. This view is, however, implicitly opposed to the classical view which regarded instincts as perfect *ab initio* and accordingly unmodifiable; such instincts being held to constitute an all-sufficient guide for conduct in the more important affairs of life, and thus to afford an efficient substitute for reason, the prerogative of man and the gods.

This latter view, only rendered possible through inadequate observation and neglect of subsequent verification by appeal to the facts of nature, has now been consigned to the limbo of myths. But although it has, perforce, had to be abandoned, the science of animal psychology is not as yet in a position to lay down a final theory of instinctive behaviour. It is true, however, an assertion has been lately made that the separation of instinct and intelligence is a purely artificial act of abstraction—'instinct regarded from within becomes intelligence ; intelligence regarded from without becomes instinct ' —briefly, that instinct and intelligence are but two aspects of one and the same process, the former aspect, however, being more prominent in what are called instincts, the latter aspect being more prominent in so-called intelligent activity.

Realising the foolishness of attempting to make bricks without straw, attention has of late been principally directed to a more extended observation of conduct in general and of so-called instinctive behaviour in particular. Nor has this re-examination of the facts proved vain ; for it has yielded a mass of evidence clearly demonstrating the fallible nature of instincts, and in so doing has given the death-blow to the older theory. Moreover, the infallible nature of instincts once disproved, they are to a large extent denuded of their mystery and reduced to the level of the other phenomena of conduct, thus becoming possible and necessary objects of scientific investigation.

Now this very *fallibility or imperfection* of instincts in itself constitutes a most interesting problem for the student of behaviour. Is there any apparent reason, is there any common principle underlying the various cases where instinct appears in the guise of a blind leader? Let us examine a few instances chosen at random.

As is well known, the flesh-fly occasionally lays its eggs (to their ultimate destruction) on the flowers of the carrion-plant instead of on putrid flesh. Again, the *Sitaris* beetle when in its larval condition must become attached to a bee or perish; nevertheless, the larvae are not endowed with the power to recognise the bee as such, but only with the tendency to seek attachment to any hairy object which comes within reach, and it appears that 'they attach themselves with equal readiness to any other hairy insect.' An ant, *Tetramorium cespitum*, has the custom of laying its eggs in small depressions; but this tendency leads them sadly astray, as they will deposit them with equal readiness in front of the brood-parasite, the *Clythra* larva. Even in birds a somewhat similar phenomenon may be noted. Craig, who has carefully analysed the various

calls of pigeons, finds that the nest-call which
is usually given in the nest for the purpose
of calling the other mate back to it, may also
be given when the bird is in the hollow of one's
hand: in fact he writes ' hollow places have
for the ring-dove somewhat the same suggestive
power as a nest.' And lastly we may instance
the case of mating, where, in view of its biological
importance, we might most confidently look
for a specific correspondence between the instinctive activity and the object of its satisfaction
But even here it has been shown that there is
no infallible recognition of the female as such.
For example, Pearse writes that 'during the
mating season the male crawfish turns over every
crawfish that comes its way, the males often
attempt to copulate with individuals of their
own sex and the method is one of trial.' Holmes
also found that an amphipod would carry about
a decapitated male which exerted no resistance,
just as readily as a passive female.

Now an examination of these cases will
serve to reveal several important results. In
the first place it will be quite clear that in the
instances cited there is *no recognition of individualised stimuli as such ;* there is only a response
to a single stimulus or at most to an aggregation

of simple stimuli. Thus the behaviour of the flesh-fly is best explained by the assumption that oviposition is determined, not by putrid flesh or by carrion-plant *per se*, but simply by a certain chemical stimulus more or less similar in the two cases. With the *Sitaris* larva we cannot but suppose that it is the common quality 'hairiness' which determines, and alone suffices to provoke, the response. Corresponding explanations will readily suggest themselves in the remaining instances. In no case does the animal recognise the object which prompts the instinctive action as a single, specific, individualised object; it responds rather to certain qualities, qualities which, it frequently happens, are common to many different objects, while the remaining qualities characterising the object in question are ignored. In fact, the purely instinctive animal neglects differences, even those having a vital significance for it. Anything more or less closely resembling the normal adequate stimulus will serve to elicit the instinctive action, no matter how varied and diverse its concomitants may be (provided of course that none of the concomitants constitutes an adequate stimulus to an opposed instinctive action). And for this reason instinct has been called blind; because it responds at once, given the adequate conditions, without observing the possible warning accompaniments.

Before passing on, however, it may be well to point out that, although the stimulus of an instinct is generalised, yet the property or properties evoking the instinctive response are, as a rule, such as will be most frequently met with in a setting appropriate to such response. For example, a hen would normally very seldom encounter firm, bright, light oval objects other than its own eggs; therefore in the majority of cases the incubating response would be the most suitable. The amphipod does not habitually come across decapitated males of its own species. *T. cespitum* will find more depressions suitable for nests than are situated in front of the destroyer *Clythra*; and were it not so, the species must gradually suffer extinction.

The fact of the absence of any specific correspondence between instinctive activity and the object eliciting it has yet another, and highly important, aspect in that it makes experimentation possible, while it may, at the same time, assume the *rôle* of ingenuity. Suppose, for example, that certain birds should be endowed with instincts so specific in character as to refuse to build their nests save with one particular kind of moss or twig : it is conceivable that in such an event the nest would not infrequently have to go unbuilt on account of the dearth of the particular material in question.   Very different is the case at Soleure, the centre of a big watch-making industry, where nests largely constructed of the cast-away mechanism of watches are repeatedly found.   Similarly as regards the position of the nest ; with a rigorously specific instinct many nesting-places now proving useful and convenient, such as the inside of a pan, the crevice of a pipe, etc., would have to be passed by.   The moral scarcely needs pointing out, for it is obvious that the more generalised the instinct, the greater the chance of its finding an outlet.   And it is in view of this truth that the aberrations of instinct have been termed ' useful errors.'

This leads us to another consideration, namely, that of the *modifiability* of instinct.   Take an animal with generalised instincts that by the exigencies of the environment is led to experiment, then provided that such an animal is able to profit by experience it is given an opportunity to modify its instinctive responses in accordance with its individual needs.   A somewhat different manner in which modification may be brought about, though one that still depends on the generalised character of instincts, is well illustrated by the reactions produced by fear. The 'fear disposition' with its divers effects would appear to be one of the most generalised of all instincts. And the value of its generality is evident, since it is not only a particular species or class of situations which is to be feared, but within one and the same species it frequently happens that certain individuals alone are harmful and are therefore to be picked out from their fellows as objects of fear. Now in such a state of affairs it is difficult to conceive any mode of inheritable mechanism which would invariably insure the correct response. Frequently the adequate object of fear can only be determined through experience. Hence we find Kuhlmann writing : 'An animal will fear and continue to fear instinctively everything for which it has no great use, or for which there are no special causes for not avoiding'; and again, 'reactions to fear are purely instinctive in their origin, affected by experience only on the side of inhibition.'

Clearly this generalised nature of instinctive response, when associated with ability to profit by

the results of experience, admits of a much nicer
and finer adaptation than would be possible
with a more specifically individualised stimulus.

Under certain conditions the instinctive response may become even more generalised.
This is seen to advantage in those instincts
which are most closely associated with the
imperative needs of the organism. Now these,
as is well known, unless in due course they
find an outlet, render the subject increasingly
restless and intractable until such time as they
meet with satisfaction or finally wane through
want of it. But it appears that, within certain
limits, the longer the instinct is kept unsatisfied,
the more insistent it becomes, and the less
particular about the object of satisfaction; the
object, in fact, becomes increasingly generalised
until, in some cases, the instinctive response
may be given in quite unsuitable conditions.
Such behaviour, it will be convenient to speak
of as the *extension of instinctive response.*
Possibly the flesh-fly's response to the carrion-
plant should come under this category. Objects,
which normally would elicit no response, will,
if the instinct is kept unsatisfied, receive the
response usually denied. The response, however,
is not given with equal readiness to any object,

but its range is only gradually extended, first
to objects closely resembling the appropriate
one and then, by degrees, to those less similar.
We may here see an analogy with the hungry
actinian, for whereas this animal when nearly
sated cannot be induced to seize blotting-paper
soaked in meat-juice, refusing everything save
meat, the hungry individual will eagerly grasp
the less appetizing morsel; moreover, the state
of its hunger can be to some extent gauged
by the weakness of the solution to which it will
respond. Dismissing analogies and turning to
actual examples—the writer has more than once
had hen-canaries who would sit on clay eggs
until their own were laid, whereupon they
invariably proceeded to turn the clay eggs
(and those only) out of the nest. Of especial
interest, however, are the careful observations
made by Breed in regard to the drinking reaction
in chicks. It seems that the drinking reaction
as contrasted with the pecking reaction, usually
begins as 'the result of a contact stimulation
mediated by the prior activity of the pecking
and imitating instincts'; *i.e.* that while contact of the beak with water, etc., will occasion
swallowing, such contact is apparently only
brought about by accident, as by the chick

pecking at a grain in water, at watery excrement, or by seeing another chick drinking. But Breed found that when chicks after hatching were kept without water for three days the behaviour was different. For not only did accidental contact with water, brought about in the ways just mentioned, occasion swallowing, but further under these conditions the mere sight of water or of objects bearing a superficial resemblance to it, such as glazed kymograph-paper, smooth white notepaper or the edge of a glass dish, sufficed to call forth the first two movements of the characteristic drinking reaction ; and this without any previous experience of drinking. These ' observations show that if the need be sufficiently urgent a large variety of objects ...elicit the action.' The utility is obvious.

What clearly emerges from the preceding account is that in instinct, as usually understood, there are two aspects to be distinguished : there is the impulse and the satisfaction of the impulse. As we have seen, the failure of instinct in the foregoing cases is due to the lack of appropriate material (e.g. food, water, etc.) and to the consequent apparent blunting of recognition which follows; failure of the impulse, on the contrary, occurs but seldom, and then only under abnormal conditions or in pathological cases. It is indisputable that it is the impulse which is the really important matter, for, so long as this exists, it will seek satisfaction until, perhaps, eventually it accidentally encounters a suitable object; but where the impulse is absent, there, too, the instinct is lacking. It is the impulse that truly constitutes the instinct.

Now this suggests another important fact, namely, that an instinct is not merely an immediate, direct response to a simple stimulus; hence it is not a reflex. Indeed, in instinctive as contrasted with reflex action, the response is frequently indirect; for example, a hungry organism becomes restless and hunts about, but the true response to hunger is the seizing and swallowing of food—not the long search for it. Consider too, the behaviour of birds when engaged in nest-building. Brief observation will suffice to show that, in the majority of cases, when no materials are at hand birds will go in search of them. Moreover, the instinct is not satisfied by the mere finding, picking up and haphazard removal of the material, but we find a tendency displayed to convey it to a certain locality—not different bits to different areas—regardless of the direction from which it was obtained, until at length the structure is complete. And this implies a unity of purpose running throughout, a unity which it is difficult, if not impossible, to explain in terms of pure reflexes or tropisms, however complex the hypothesis. Nor must instincts proper be confused with mere chains of reflexes, since, in some cases at least, the customary order of events may be transposed— a wasp that generally digs its nest before going in search of prey to provision the same, may, at times, reverse the procedure.

The chief feature of interest, however, is that the instinctive response seems to be independent of any external stimulus; in other words it is *self-dependent*. If the proper environment is not present the animal will, nevertheless, endeavour to perform its instinctive actions, despite their thorough unsuitability to the surroundings. Thus it is that we get perverted instincts, *e.g.* the sucking instinct. And in cases where the environment is such that it is impossible for the activity to manifest itself, the instinct tends in general to lapse and become evanescent. Kittens of five months when presented with mice for the first time appeared quite indifferent and certainly exhibited no

trace of any killing instinct.   Yerkes and Bloom-
field found, however, distinct traces of this
instinct in kittens from one to two months
old, and ascribe the former results to the waning
of the instinct through disuse.

Now the fact that, at times, instinct will
endeavour to find satisfaction, even in the
absence of any suitable extra-organic stimulus,
and *vice versâ*, leads us to ask what it is that
arouses the inherited disposition to activity ?
Why does potential building-material, which
is neglected during the greater part of the year,
suddenly become interesting to birds ?   Since
nest-building is instinctive it follows that it
must be an inherited disposition, and therefore .always present.   Why then are birds not
equally disposed at all seasons of the year to
pick up twigs, etc., and mould them into a nest ?
The only reason that can be educed to explain
the varying behaviour is that the disposition
in question is not always functioning, but from
time to time lapses into latency.

Now the problem before us consists in
determining the conditions under which an
inherited disposition becomes functional. Broadly
it may be said to depend upon the setting,
i.e. upon the physiological state of the organism.

The disposition to appease hunger, as distinguished from mere *gourmandise*, only occurs in certain conditions of metabolism. In other words, whether the instinctive disposition shall function or remain inactive is here determined by the chemical state of the organism. And it is on similar lines that we must look for an explanation of the so-called periodic instincts, such as nest-building. Fortunately it is possible to point with more or less certainty to an efficient cause.

Of the periodic instincts those concerned with reproduction are by far the most important. At the pairing season of the year a complete change may be observed in the habits and behaviour of many species; the rutting stag, for example, is a keen fighter easily provoked, though at other times peaceable enough; the *Molge palmatus* newt, ordinarily a land-dweller, takes to water at the breeding season. In both instances the structures necessary to the performance of the activity in question—antlers in the one case and a web connecting the toes of the hind feet in the other—only come into existence as the sexual organs become active, disappearing again in the sterile stage. Now it is known that the reproductive, like some

other glands, secrete, when active, certain chemical bodies or hormones. And the view generally
held is that the aforesaid structural changes
are stimulated, and to a large extent regulated,
by this internal secretion, which, formed by
the sexual glands, is absorbed into the blood
and so circulated to various parts of the body.
But the point of real interest to us is that, in
all likelihood, it is these same sexual hormones
which incite to functional activity the instinctive
dispositions of which the secondary structures
referred to act as the instrument.

The foregoing considerations serve also to
demonstrate the significance of the *action-system*.
Newts cannot swim efficiently without the
requisite apparatus, nor do they, apparently,
manifest any desire to take to water in the
seasons intervening between the breeding seasons,
when the web is no longer present. Indeed,
at this stage of evolution instinct and structure,
in the majority of cases, must have arrived at
some sort of balance ; thus it comes about that
the behaviour manifested is generally adapted
to the structure shown. And so the way is
opened up to an understanding of the varied,
even opposed, lines of conduct exhibited by an
animal at different stages of metamorphosis.

Granted that the fertilized egg, which develops into the crawling, gnawing caterpillar and, later, into the flitting, honey-sucking butterfly, is endowed with inherited dispositions corresponding to all the varieties of instinctive behaviour displayed, still, despite the co-existence of such contrasted dispositions, no confusion or useless conflict results; each mode of behaviour, while it is necessary and suitable to the corresponding stage of growth, is as transitory as the structure or system to which it is adapted. The various dispositions become functional in due sequence, lapsing into latency again when some new modification renders them useless or harmful. It is tempting to see here a relationship akin to that which exists between antagonistic reflexes, and to suppose that the functioning of one disposition inhibits that of another opposed disposition. Such a supposition is, however, mere conjecture; moreover the mechanism at all events must be very different in the two cases; in the latter it might conceivably have a chemical base.

Instincts which are not manifested at birth but only appear later, after their appropriate structures have been developed, are known as ' *deferred* ' instincts. An excellent example

of both a transitory and a deferred instinct
is to be found in the nuptial flight of ants.
This does not take place until the males and
females are thoroughly mature; up to that
time, and after the flight, their life is terrestrial.

We have had reason to insist upon the
intimate relation between instinct and structure.
This relationship has suggested to some writers
the possibility that such improvement in accuracy,
in delicacy of adjustment and of motor-co-
ordination,—in fact all those changes which
mark the gradual progress from the ' self-
contained ' but at first somewhat inefficient
reaction—is not, in reality, to be attributed
to the effects of exercise but can be adequately
accounted for on purely structural grounds.
Such a contention admits, to some extent,
of verification or disproof by means of observation and experiment; and various observations
have been directed to this end though, as yet,
without yielding any conclusive evidence sub-
stantiating either a categorical affirmation or
denial.

What does appear fairly decisively, however,
is that a certain degree of ' skill ' in the employ-
ment of an instinctive activity may be acquired
in the absence of exercise of the activity in

question. Kuhlmann has noticed, for instance, that whereas some nestlings on first leaving the nest can fly only a few feet, others manage as much as a distance of one hundred yards, the difference depending on whether they leave the nest a few days early or late. Somewhat analogous too, are Craig's observations on the pigeon's coo. He finds the coo very 'variable in the time of its appearance'; usually 'it is extremely imperfect and does not in the least suggest the sound it is to assume,' but 'it seems that in those individuals in which the coo appears very late, it is correspondingly well developed when it does appear'; and he concludes 'there are reasons for believing that practice has very little effect in developing the voice of the dove.' Much the same would seem to hold true also of man; for it appears that the enunciation of children whose speech is delayed is frequently remarkably clear and well defined, and that in such cases the usual period of word or 'sound-stumbling' is greatly shortened, if not entirely omitted.

It would appear, therefore, that some instinctive activities may proceed, at any rate some small way, towards perfection apart from practice. But that practice is ineffective and entirely

superfluous is by no means proved. For, first, as we
have already seen, certain instincts in the absence
of conditions necessary to their exercise gradually
wane, tending to lapse completely in course of
time. And, secondly, Breed, in some experiments
especially designed to test the importance of
exercise in developing, perfecting, and so to
speak, adding the finishing touch to instinct,
found that ' so far as the facts are concerned,
the most that one can say is that the development of the pecking instinct proceeds somewhat
without practice and is hastened by it. Maturation and use run along in time together.' The
observations from which this conclusion was
deduced were as follows :—Two sets of chicks
were compared in regard to the accuracy of
their pecking capacities : the one set consisted
of five birds allowed to feed normally from the
time of hatching ; the other, of three birds
of the same age, but which from the outset
were confined in a dark-box. The chicks of
this latter group, in which pecking was artificially
deferred, were given their first pecking test
in the light some forty hours later. Though
no noteworthy difference in the physical development of the two sets could be detected, it, nevertheless, appeared to Breed that on the whole

'(1) the development of the instinct was retarded
by disuse, and that (2) the retardation was
quickly overcome with use.' These results have
been corroborated by subsequent tests of a more
extensive character. The most striking features
of the results obtained in the later investigation
were '(1) the uniformly poor initial records,
and (2) the rapidity with which normal accuracy
was attained.' The data also gave grounds
for suspecting that 'a given amount of practice,
...is necessary to smooth the way for the
operation of a native capacity whose efficiency
is largely a function of the age of the animal.'

There is then some slight show of reason
to justify the use of the term 'instinct-habit';
for though, as is quite clear, motor co-ordination
is present from the outset, even before the
neuro-muscular strength necessary to make the
movements effectively, yet the stage of final
dexterity and economy of effort, when the
subject's attention is no longer occupied by
the novelty or difficulty of the movements,
is only attained through practice and exercise.

And it is just here that we see most clearly
the relation of instinct and intelligence. For,
as instincts are not all of the same level, some
being, so to speak, much more deeply ingrained

than others, so those which are the least deeply ingrained lapse the soonest, can be most readily modified, and require a relatively greater amount of practice in order to become firmly established as habits.

CHAPTER V

HOMING

A PURELY general treatment of instinct apart from any detailed analysis of the instinctive activities is, at best, incomplete and unsatisfactory. It is therefore proposed to supplement the remarks of the preceding chapter by some account of a particular instinct, namely, homing. And this plan may be the more readily adopted in that it serves a dual purpose; for our examination, bringing to light (as it of necessity must) the importance of individual experience even within the sphere of instinct, thereby in some measure prepares the way for a consideration of the nature of animal intelligence. Incidentally too, homing affords an excellent example of the valuable results that may be achieved by field-work; while, at the same time, it serves to demonstrate the formation of associations by birds and insects under natural conditions as distinguished from the laboratory products described in an earlier chapter.

At one time the return of bees to the hive or of carrier pigeons to the cote after foraging or explorative expeditions was attributed to instinct; and this implied that the act is little short of miraculous and absolutely inexplicable. A somewhat similar view is still held by those scientists who invoke a mysterious unknown, inner or 'sixth' sense, but as will be seen later the evidence in favour of such an assumption is very slight. More and more it becomes evident that acquaintance with the position of the home—hive, nest, shell, or cote as the case may be—and the path by which return may be made, is only acquired gradually, even laboriously, by means of *individual* experience : in fact, in practically all homing reactions individual memory must play a *rôle*, and one which is by no means insignificant. It follows that all that can be properly understood by the homing 'instinct' is the basic *impulse* to regain home after absence, together with the tendency to make use of certain sense data or impressions and of associations between them, to achieve that end.

In confirmation of this view of the necessity for individual experience, certain facts may be cited. First, birds and insects appear unable

to find their way home even when quite near,
if, from youth or through removal to a strange
neighbourhood, they are unfamiliar with their
surroundings. In such cases the number of
safe returns in no wise exceeds the proportion
due to chance. Secondly, bees are said to be
unable to regain the hive in the dark. These
insects, it would seem, depend chiefly on visual
impressions and recognition of visual landmarks for finding their way: if this is not the
case, *i.e.* if they possess an unknown homing
sense, their inability to return in the dark
becomes incomprehensible. Other observations
of a similar nature agree in demonstrating
the necessity for individual acquaintance with
the environment.

It is possible to go farther, and to point,
in some cases at least, to the mode by which
such experience is probably acquired. We start
with the fundamental fact that, in general,
animals taken from their home and placed in
new and unfamiliar surroundings rarely succeed
in returning, at any rate directly and immediately.
Thus, in the majority of cases it is actually true
to speak of the return journey as a function
of the outgoing. As the animal travels outwards,
its various receptors are constantly receiving

' impressions ' from external and internal stimuli, impressions which, like all others, produce a modification lasting a certain time. In consequence, when the animal reverses and starts homeward-bound, it is more or less attuned to a certain sequence of impressions; and novel stimuli, striking discordantly, are avoided, possibly because of the feeling of strangeness and uneasiness they produce. Through this avoidance of the novel and unfamiliar it comes about that the return journey is in some sense controlled, the animal being more or less negatively guided and kept to the path by which the goal may be reached.

It is obvious, however, that the transitory memory just described is only rudimentary in character and admits of considerable development as regards both permanence (duration) and extent. At the higher stages it is not necessary in order to insure return that the animal shall have just recently made the outward journey. Even such a relatively lowly creature as the limpet may retain a working recognition of the environment extending to a distance of 10 cms. from its ' scar ' or temporary home, over a period of two weeks, and a similar retentiveness is shown by many species of ants.

As regards extent, it has been found that bees conveyed under cover to a spot several kilometers distant from the hive, return thither almost directly upon release, provided that the zone is already familiar ; while in carrier pigeons, as is well known, this ability is very highly developed.

Considerable light has been thrown of late on the nature of this topographical knowledge, by such patient and painstaking investigators as Turner, Buttel-Reepen, and the Peckhams.

Impressions of the trail or district, received through the receptors, are almost, if not always, indispensable, and may be regarded as furnishing ' cues.' The cues, however, vary according to the conditions and the species. To the overlooking of this fact must be attributed the hopeless confusion which for so long has characterised the whole subject. It is illegitimate to predicate what has been found true for one particular variety as true for the whole species or genus. To take an instance : the *Lasius* ant, an insect with an ill-developed eye, seems to rely mainly on odours and tactile sensations for guidance, alterations in these stimuli causing marked disturbance, while changes in any other stimuli apparently pass unnoticed. Its explorations are

limited to a comparatively small area, and on its
return it follows almost precisely the outgoing
trail. Very different, on the other hand, is the
behaviour of such ants as the *Formicae* and
Polyergi; in their case a tendency to cut off
détours and sinuosities is evident on the return
journey, so that the centripetal path rarely
coincides with the centrifugal, being usually more
direct. Confusion, too, and disturbance are
seldom manifested except on the removal of
such outstanding features of the neighbourhood
as probably serve to afford visual landmarks.

In the case of many of the Hymenoptera
it is now possible to point out with some degree
of certainty the receptors that furnish them
with their main cues. But it must be borne
in mind that the predominance of, and customary
reliance on, one class of cues by no means excludes
the use of others derived through different
receptors. For example, Santschi writes of a
N. African ant—'the trace of odour is not sufficient to explain fully the orientation of the ants
that follow it [the trail] and it is supplemented
by means of contact ideas.' Such auxiliary
cues, however, are generally subordinate and
probably remain more or less unnoticed until,
some alteration in the conditions rendering

the normal cues ineffectual or unavailable,
the animal is forced to resort to other aids.
Thus Burrill has found that one of the slave-
making ants, *F. sanguinea*, normally follows the
trail by smell, but that smell on occasion may
be superseded by sight. Watson likewise finds
that noddy terns do not use visual factors ex-
clusively in the return to the nest; for, on disturbance of these, the birds apparently make use
of a 'locality' or 'position' factor.

It would seem that the class of cues most
universally depended on in case of failure of
the normal cues, is that afforded by internal
stimuli derived from the movements of the
body, etc. Piéron tells us that whereas the
limpet relies mainly on impressions derived
through the tactile end-organs, yet on the failure
of these, due to alteration of the rock surface,
it is efficiently guided by presumably kinaesthetic
factors; while the *Lasius* ant, according to the
same writer, exhibits closely similar behaviour
on the alteration or obliteration of 'chemical'
cues. Such facts recall the handing over of
control from one set of cues to another, already
described, in the learning of a maze by rodents
and other animals.

This substitution of internal for external

cues has not only a temporal aspect, as manifested in the gradual automatization of a series of movements frequently repeated, but also a spatial aspect. In other words when the area constantly explored by an animal is fairly wide, it normally falls into two zones, an inner one nearer home which is smaller, better-known and necessarily more frequently traversed, and an outer one of greater extent with which the subject is in consequence less familiar. Santschi notes, for instance, that certain ants on return waver at first, but proceed more directly as the neighbourhood of the nest is approached; their behaviour suggests an evident familiarity with the immediate approach. There is much evidence to show that in the inner zone so-called 'muscular' memory is supreme, though it is unavailing in the outer zone. If this presumption is valid, moreover, it goes far to explain certain facts hitherto presenting troublesome anomalies. Some of these we may proceed to examine.

It is now acknowledged that a superior homing capacity is usually correlated with dependence upon visual cues predominantly. Many of the solitary wasps, notably *Sphex* and *Cerceris*, prior to leaving their nest on its

completion in search of provision, make elaborate
and systematic locality studies. They circle
round the nest several times, approaching and
again flying farther away, so 'making a detailed
study of every little object near the nest'
(fig. 8). It is said that they are engaged in

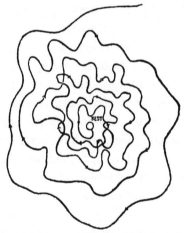

Fig. 8. Thorough locality study by *Sphex*.
(After G. W. and E. G. Peckham.)

getting their bearings by acquiring a visual
impression of the nest and its *entourage*; no
like care is shown apparently in the case of
nests deserted before completion. Most bees
also make a similar careful examination of their

surroundings on leaving the hive for the first
time. It is asserted that should this preliminary
survey be suppressed or prevented the insects
are seldom able to find their way home. In
young birds the immature muscular development compels slow and gradual learning of the
environment of the nest. The marvellous feats
accomplished by the carrier pigeon are largely
due to careful and systematic artificial training.
The young bird is taken from the cote and
first released in a familiar zone, and then subsequently at gradually increasing distances.

As regards proof of the statement that visual
landmarks are of supreme importance in the
aforementioned cases, it has been found that
pigeons, bees, and wasps alike are disconcerted
by alteration or removal of such outstanding
features of the environment as may be supposed
to serve as visual *points de repère*. Thus,
one wasp, *Aporus fasciatus*, entirely lost her
way when a leaf covering the nest was broken
off, but found it again at once as soon as the
leaf was replaced. Bouvier made the following
tests with *Bembex* : he hid her nest with a flat
stone whereupon the wasp showed signs of
disturbance, circling above the nest once or twice
before alighting. During her next absence the

stone was removed to a distance of 2 decimeters ; on return *Bembex* alighted at once on the stone and sought the nest, and although twice chased away she returned and continued the search. On the stone being replaced in its original position *Bembex* at once found the entrance. The literature of the subject abounds with similar instances. After any such change in the immediate surroundings of the nest the bee or wasp, thereby temporarily disoriented, makes a new survey of the locality of the most careful character before again setting out on an expedition.

So much for one class of cases. Of no less interest, however, are another set of observations yielding results which stand in sharp contrast to the above. According to the indications furnished by this second class of instances, the removal of outstanding landmarks from the *immediate* vicinity seems to pass unnoticed, and this too in insects that rely for guidance, over a greater part of the area traversed, upon cues furnished by visual stimuli! Thus in one experiment where the entrance to the hive was completely disguised by dead branches the bees still flew direct to it, nor did they seem one whit disconcerted. Even when the gum itself was removed to a spot 2 kilometers distant and well in sight, these bees, unlike *Bembex* which relies on recognition of the landmark—plant or stone—rather than on pure positional memory as such, flew to the exact position originally occupied by the gum, where they continued to hover about, obviously desiring their home yet never approaching it, prominent object as it was. It seems clear that in the two last cases the use of visual *points de repère* has been superseded in the inner and more familiar zone by a partially automatic type of behaviour, that is accompanied by a remarkable memory for position.

Of the existence of an absolute positional memory, as well of its dominance and tenacity in innumerable species from the monkeys downwards, there is ample evidence, as experimenters know to their cost. And it now appears to be a phenomenon not less well-established in certain bees. Indeed, many of these insects show a marvellously accurate memory, not only for the exact height of the opening of the hive from the ground, but also for the position of the entrance, so that the latter is seldom found if the hive be slightly revolved. Equally astonishing is the memory displayed for the precise

position of the hive itself; while even honey
or a flower once visited may so dominate memory
that a bee winging its way thither will completely
ignore honey placed close to the line of flight,
in a situation where normally it would immediately claim attention. In solitary wasps,
on the other hand, the memory of absolute
position is comparatively rare.

Now the significance of this is obvious.
For whereas the hive bee has a more or less
permanent home, the solitary wasp is constantly
seeking pastures new; one nest is no sooner
completed than she flies off to start another
in a different locality. Under such conditions
the home is at best nothing more than a passing
pied-à-terre. Such an existence scarcely favours
the development of stereotyped habits and
pure positional memory; indeed, the possession
of the latter would constitute a drawback
rather than otherwise. Moreover, the greatest
degree of positional memory among wasps is
exhibited by *Bembex*, and it is significant that
her home is somewhat more permanent, for she
differs from many other wasps in feeding her
young from day to day.

It has been objected that, even granting
the existence of such highly developed positional

memory, and admitting the ability of the insects
in question to find their way home in a *quasi-*
mechanical manner, the apparent failure to
note the absence of the one important detail
of the situation, *e.g.* the hive, is still left un-
explained.   Unfortunately this difficulty can only
be met by conjectures.   Consider the case where
the hive is removed but a very short distance,
remaining well in view from the old position.
The bees return as usual and hover about, never,
it is affirmed, noticing the hive.   But is it not
possible that, in an insect dominated by positional
memory, the hive is so altered by its change of
position that it becomes *ipso facto* a new object,
constituting at most a disturbing feature and
having for the subject no relation whatsoever
to the old familiar home?   In other words,
change of situation probably carries with it
an entire change in meaning.   Take the case
of *Bembex* : it lives for the most part in a semi-
social state, the nests of different individuals
being only an inch or two apart ; further, a
district markedly devoid of landmarks such
as a plain sandy soil, is generally selected.
Yet out of the numerous burrows, differing to
the human observer only as regards position,
' *Bembex* swoops down upon the exact spot

at which the entrance to her nest is hidden '
with ' unerring accuracy,' though a stranger
wasp excavating a nest among a *Bembex* colony
is utterly unable to find it on return and
runs in and out of the various *Bembex* holes.
We must conclude that here at least meaning
attaches solely to the position occupied.

On taking facts of this nature into consideration, it ceases to be surprising that the bees
fail to go to the hive in its new position. To do
so would imply the ability to recognise similarity
in difference, a power of abstraction which their
general conduct gives us no warrant to conclude.

The fact that the bees continue to hover
over the deserted spot, instead of at once flying
off and scouring the neighbourhood for their
goal, also, has occasioned a certain amount
of surprise. Reflexion will show, however,
that such conduct is consonant with the rest
of their behaviour. The general vicinity, save
for the absence of one feature, remains unchanged.
In all probability, therefore, coming as it does
as the last of a sequence of experiences customarily leading to the desired goal, and thus
exciting a certain measure of preparedness for it,
it is recognised by the bees. To go farther and
marvel that the insects do not immediately

notice the absence of the hive and at once seek
for it, is to neglect the distinction between
recognition and recollection, a distinction which
unfortunately has not always been sufficiently
borne in mind by writers on this subject.

This apparent contrast between the recognition of the permanent zone and the visual
memory of particular objects within it, which at
first glance seems so unique, suggests yet another
distinction that must be drawn, *viz.*, one between the characters of the visual cues employed.
This distinction, though largely relative, is by no
means devoid of interest. It seems that while
many creatures rely for guidance in this sphere
chiefly upon detail, others, over a large part of
their course at least, appear to make use of what
may be termed, as contrasted with detail, visual
ensemble. It is stated, for instance, that, in
those ants which rely chiefly on sight, all modification of the path is without effect. Topographical
memory embraces a large field in which details
are of relatively slight value. In consequence,
these ants are seldom lost and their mode of
orientation permits them a considerable degree
of latitude. Often, too, insects that are ' put
out' by the removal or alteration of certain
details of the environment fly aloft and so are

able to get their bearings once more from the general *ensemble*. It is practically certain that in creatures whose beat takes in a large area, *ensemble* is relied on in the districts more remote from home, even though detail is paramount in the inner zone. A typical instance is the homing of carrier pigeons, which must now be examined

Clearly, from the point of view of vision, animals endowed with the power of flight have an advantage over their earth-bound relatives; and, within limits, the higher the flight the greater the advantage. Everyone knows the clear, schematic relief of the so-called 'bird's-eye' view. Prominent objects, such as mountains, can be seen from afar, are possibly recognised, and may serve as cues to birds many miles distant : in this way actual first-hand acquaintance with the environment ceases to be absolutely indispensable, a fact which helps to explain the marvellous returns of carrier pigeons from points far beyond their normal range after being conveyed thither in closed baskets. For the difference in results, according as pigeons are permitted to observe the country through which they are passing or not, has been placed beyond doubt. It demonstrates the immense value of visual landmarks to these birds.

Other theories are still put forward to account for the homing of pigeons. They differ very much in value. The telepathy hypothesis, for instance, since telepathy itself remains non-proven, may be at once rejected. Of what use to endeavour to explain the unknown by the equally, if not still more, unknown? The theory of a magnetic sense, contended for by Thauziès, can scarcely claim serious attention in the absence of any critical experiments: the *onus probandi* at present lies with its advocates.

But there remain other hypotheses which cannot be so summarily dismissed. After all, homing is a very complex phenomenon; and, although the use of visual landmarks plays an important *rôle*, it does not follow that the participation of other factors in the reaction is excluded. It is not improbable, for example, that the so-called labyrinthine memory (which is due to impressions received through the semi-circular canals, together possibly with those from the utricle and saccule, being the end organs which passively register angular and linear displacement respectively) may in some small means afford an auxiliary cue; it may, in fact, partially account for the safe returns of birds loosed on sea out

of sight of land where the change of direction
is rare. Labyrinthine memory has also been put
forward, with less cogency, to explain the isolated
cases of the well-nigh miraculous returns of
dogs and cats to their old home after having
been transported to a distant part of the
country by rail. At best, however, it constitutes but a partial explanation. Moreover,
such memory is inoperative in young birds,
where, if anywhere, we should expect to find
it supreme, since being untainted by experience
they are not likely to be influenced to the same
degree as adults by misleading associations
or visual impressions.

Claim has also been made that, in the absence
of other cues, guidance may be furnished by
the direction of the wind, the position of the
sun's rays, etc. But it is obvious that factors
such as these can only be of limited value to
pigeons, whether Santschi is right in asserting
that ' solar tropism ' is of foremost importance
in the case of certain ants or not. In this
connexion it may not be amiss to mention
that the direction of currents has been invoked
to explain the migration of fishes ; but this
is a realm in which too little work has been
done.

There remains for consideration the so-
called ' inner sense,' or sense of direction.   Now
of the receptors of this sense nothing is known.
But the mass of evidence accumulating in recent
years renders imperative a more serious examination of the facts alleged.   At first the postulation of an inner sense was little better than a con-
fession of ignorance.   How explain otherwise, it
was asked, the safe return of pigeons loosed on
sea out of sight of land, or indeed of any object
serving as a *point de repère* ?   Of three noddy
terns released in mid-ocean two returned 460
miles in three days.   These birds also when
sent north returned a distance of 1000 miles
along an unfamiliar coast, despite the fact
that they had never before been more than
15 knots distant from the land in that direction.
So far the hypothesis of an inner sense is nothing
more than idle conjecture, but it changes to
something more substantial in the case of
the Hymenoptera, especially ants.

Cornetz, as the result of his recent elaborate
observations on five species of N. African ants
which forage singly, asserts that they possess
an extraordinary faculty of maintaining their
course in a definite direction.   The direction
adopted by the insect on leaving the nest is

definitely resumed after each of the many
interruptions, whether these are due to the
intervention of the observer, to being carried
out of her course by the wind or to the insect's
own exploratory tendencies; deviations of the
latter kind reach as many as ten or twelve
on a single outward journey and are themselves
frequently very complex, consisting of many
loops and turns. This ability to resume a given
direction has been described by Cornetz as 'the
constant reappearance of the once impressed
wandering direction.' A further complication
is found in the fact that 'sometimes the insect
outward bound adopts successively two directions,
often at right angles to each other, and on her
return retraces them successively in inverse
order.' But this behaviour must not be confused with mere muscular memory. The return
is not due to a kinematic reverse of the movements made on the outward journey, as Piéron
affirms of *Aphaenogaster* (though Turner dis-
agrees). As a matter of fact, in the N. African
ants under consideration, the sequence of the
actual movements performed on the return
journey, as well as the route traversed, has
been found at times to differ very considerably
from that observed on the outgoing path.

At most Cornetz would reduce the *rôle* of muscular
memory in the species examined to that of a
pedometer giving a very *rough* estimate of the
distance travelled. But even within these modified limits muscular memory does not appear
to afford a very reliable guide; over and over
again the ants stop much too soon and commence
the characteristic turning, always given in the
vicinity of the nest and generally known as
the '*tournoiement de Turner.*' For guidance
by muscular memory, therefore, Cornetz would
substitute an innate ability to maintain and
follow a given direction—not, be it carefully
noted, a trail. And this ability which does
not depend on sight, smell, touch, or movement,
or in fact on any cue yet analysed, is ascribed
to an ' inner sense.'

Nor are the facts related by Cornetz absolutely
unique, forming a class apart, since observations
pointing to the same conclusion have been
recorded quite independently. Thus Hardy
finds that a certain wasp, *Diamma bicolor*,
when dragging her prey home has constantly
to leave it in order to reconnoitre; on returning,
however, she always goes forward in the same
general direction. And Andrews, without having
obtained definite experimental evidence, thinks

that the behaviour of termites also points to the possession of a similar, though much more rudimentary, sense of direction. Bonnier's experiments were rather different. Their outcome proved that bees are able to distinguish between two directions which differ from one another by an exceedingly small angle ; and this, he claims, can only be explained on the assumption of the presence of a very delicate sense of direction.

Whether there are really grounds for demanding the postulation of sensations of direction obtained by individual experience but independently of any of the known receptors, it is impossible as yet to say. What does emerge clearly is the necessity for further investigation.

CHAPTER VI

IMITATION

Two main types of imitation are usually distinguished, the one being described as instinctive, the other as inferential or reflective. These two sub-classes are, however, widely different; and their subsumption under the same general class must be attributed to the objective resemblance between their respective phenomena, rather than to any underlying subjective relationship between the processes involved. Indeed, the former type, as its name implies, is more properly considered in connexion with instinct, while the latter, presumably a much higher type, necessitates an investigation of the level of general intelligence. Hence a consideration of the various actions classed under imitation, forcing on us as it does a transition from generally unreflective behaviour to the highest levels of animal intelligence, may conveniently find place here.

In instinctive imitation, as usually understood, there need be no definite intention on
the part of the imitator to copy the action
of the imitatee or to achieve a similar result.
The *sine qua non* is that the imitatee's action
shall serve as a stimulus calling forth similar
behaviour in its companions, such behaviour
following almost reflexly (or instinctively) upon
the perception of the original performance.
The well-known tendency to yawn when in
company with a yawner affords an excellent
illustration. In other words instinctive behaviour may be elicited, not only by its appropriate stimulus but also, in the absence of
that stimulus, by the instinctive action of other
animals. Hachet-Souplet reports, for instance,
that pigeons placed in one compartment of a
cage and deprived of food will, nevertheless,
proceed to peck the floor vigorously on perceiving
their neighbours in the adjoining compartment
pecking corn.

Recognition of the existence of this so-
called instinctive imitation has been followed
by an exaggerated idea of its importance.
Writers have spoken of a definite imitating
'instinct,' and it has been argued that the
possession of such an instinct, leading an animal

to copy the behaviour of other members of
its species, renders unnecessary the inheritance
of more specific instincts and so lightens the
burden of heredity.

This view once succinctly enunciated, attention has been naturally directed to the behaviour
of young animals. How far, it has been asked,
is the conduct of the young imitative of their
fellows, particularly of their elders ? Do young
animals when deprived from the outset of the
companionship of older animals actually fail to
manifest any of the customary instinctive activities common to the species ? Fortunately careful
observation has done much to answer these
questions.

In the first place most writers are agreed
that, as regards instinctive imitation, only those
actions are imitated which awaken an inherited
disposition, *i.e.* an instinct, in the percipient;
in other words, that there does not, in fact,
exist a general instinct of imitation leading
an animal to copy any action whatsoever.
It follows that the assumption of an imitating
instinct does not render the inheritance of
specific instincts dispensable ; indeed, it is dependent on the latter. What it, perhaps, does
make possible is that these instincts may be

inherited in a rather more general and somewhat less stereotyped manner, thereby affording scope for increased plasticity.

Again, analysis reveals that in many of the instances cited as examples of instinctive imitation, the original action is not strictly copied, but, at most, only *suggests* another more or less similar action. An instance in point is given by Craig. He observes that young pigeons at once give a call on hearing other birds call, and that the more they hear other birds call, the more they call; yet 'they do not imitate the adults in the sense of copying them or of learning new sounds.' On the other hand, Craig does not consider it improbable that 'the calling of other birds may lead the young to give a certain sound earlier than they would give it if left alone.' This, of course, is only conjecture. But Breed actually found that the performance of the drinking reaction by one chick does seem to stimulate another chick to a similar performance, when this other chick is at the learning stage.

Breed further undertook some experiments designed with the definite object of testing the effect of social influence in increasing the accuracy of the pecking reaction in chicks.

He took two groups E and F, each comprising
six chicks, but those in group F being ten days
younger than those in group E. The chicks of
group F were placed with those of group E immediately on hatching and careful records were
taken of their pecking reactions during the first
eight days. On comparing these with the records
for the corresponding period of group E's development it was found that, despite the possible
advantage the younger chicks might derive
from stimulation by association with the older
chicks, the records showed that they 'began
less accurately than their elders, remained behind
by about the same margin during the critical
period of development, and hardly equalled
them while the experiment continued.' Further
control tests with two chicks kept in absolute
isolation gave results closely similar to those
of the chicks kept under more normal conditions ;
nor did they reveal any retardation in respect
to rapidity in consequence of the absence of
social influence.

Before returning to the examination of
instinctive imitation proper, there is one case
which, since it presents a type intermediate
between social influence and imitation, deserves
mention. A quite young monkey was placed

with an older one. The two became very friendly,
and the younger animal would constantly follow
the older one about. Not only so, but he likewise repeated the adult's actions and even
formed similar habits, such as jumping on the
experimenter's shoulder, etc. The interesting
point, however, is that the baby would never
perform any one of these actions—not even
that of coming for food—unless the older monkey
first responded. Here we do not seem to be
dealing with purely imitative behaviour. Whilst
instinctive imitation probably played a large
part, it is not unlikely that timidity and shyness
were also important factors. If this were so
it would explain the inhibition of independent
movement in the presence of the experimenter.
Possibly, too, the baby ' liked ' to be close to
the older monkey, deriving some feeling of
security from his proximity. At all events
it is significant that the young animal became
more independent as he grew older.

Another example illustrative of this intermediate type is to be found in dog-breaking ;
for, as every sportsman and shepherd knows,
by far the easiest and most rapid way of breaking
in a pup is to bring it up with well-trained
dogs.

Moreover, fundamental to both the above cases is the tendency of young animals to follow others, a fact which supplies an explanation of many phenomena which, at first sight, are attributed to instinctive imitation. A young mammal, as it follows its mother or some other animal about, is necessarily brought into contact with the same stimuli as are encountered by the latter ; and there seems no reason to suppose that these stimuli do not act *directly* upon the former, eliciting the appropriate instinctive response. What more natural, for instance, than to suppose that contact with food will of itself prompt eating ? Strictly, the most that can be urged in such cases is that the movement of the older animal may serve to attract the attention of the younger to the stimuli. That the reaction given by the second animal resembles that given by the first, may be readily accounted for on the assumption that a stimulus adapted to excite a certain inherited disposition is likely to call forth similar responses from similar organisms.

Though hitherto we have somewhat discounted the educative influence of suggestion or imitation, there are certain cases where it assumes an important *rôle*. The most notable instance is that of fear: for, whether we hold, as Kuhlmann does, that young animals at the outset fear every object save those for which they have a particular use, such as food; or whether we consider that they enter into life fearing no particular object, but only coming to acquire fear for such through association and example; it seems equally certain that the attitude of the older animals is very largely instrumental in determining the conduct of their young, both by accustoming them to harmless objects and by their regular avoidance of certain other specific objects.

On taking everything into consideration, however, it would seem that the educative influence of instinctive imitation has been unduly exaggerated in the past. In monkeys, for instance, contrary to popular belief, it appears to play no great part. Thus, of one young monkey kept under the most careful and competent observation from birth, we find it asserted 'there is no evidence to show that he ever gained a new activity by imitation.'

Nevertheless there is one form of action which, since it certainly exercises some effect as regards the acquirement of motor control, must not be omitted from our account. The behaviour in ques-

s. 9

tion is sometimes spoken of, rightly or wrongly, as self-imitation, sometimes as a circular reaction. It consists in a tendency to repeat certain movements, frequently novel movements, over and over again, and is manifested to perfection in cats and monkeys. The writer well remembers a rather backward and very heavy kitten suddenly discovering that he could, by half-scrambling, half-jumping, get on to a large table. So attractive was this new feat that the performance was repeated rapidly and without intermission as many as 200 times, after which the writer wearied of the game and the cat was removed. Next day, on the cat's return to the room, he immediately jumped on the table and continued to repeat this accomplishment until stopped.

Circular reaction or self-imitation would also seem to be an important factor in the acquiring of songs by birds. A young sparrow placed with twenty canaries gradually lost his sparrow chirp, adopting instead a song which closely resembled the confusion of notes occurring when the three adult canary songsters were singing their best. It appears that, while the ordinary call notes and narrow range of notes are hereditary, the song pattern or arrangement of notes is to a large extent due, and partially dependent upon, training. If this be true it can readily be understood that here, at least, there is room for instinctive imitation.

Sufficient has been said to show that instances of instinctive imitation undoubtedly do occur, though the phenomenon is probably much rarer than was at one time supposed. We must now inquire whether the existence in animals of any higher type of imitation can be likewise established. Is there any occasion where we are forced to conclude that an animal copies the action of another, not from a mere instinct to imitate, not even from a mere desire to reproduce the other's movements, but simply because it wishes to attain the same result ? To take an instance :—An animal is confined in a puzzle (or problem) box from which it can escape to food and freedom by working some simple mechanism (pushing aside a bolt, raising a hook, etc.). After several minutes occupied in frantic attempts to escape, our subject still fails to discover the mechanism, or at all events its mode of operation. Suppose we were now to introduce another animal familiar with the apparatus, and allow our subject to watch him successfully manipulate the fastening, would the latter profit

by the example afforded, and on the next occasion
immediately release himself in the correct fashion?
Should he indeed do so, his conduct, hinting that
the relation of means to end had been grasped,
would be strongly suggestive of inferential
imitation. It is impossible, however, to be
too careful in definitely accepting such a conclusion; for the situation contains many pit-
falls.

In the first place, it is desirable to ascertain
that subsequent success is not simply due to
the fact that the imitatee's movements have
served to attract the imitator's attention to
the important part of the box, the correct
manipulation of the fastening thereupon following
in an automatic, random, or chance manner
quite apart from any perception of its significance
in relation to the obtaining of release. Wherever
the imitator after successfully working the
mechanism fails to profit by the result of his
action, appearing oblivious to the reward or
means of escape thereby afforded, the presumption is that the relation is not apprehended.
Thus in one experiment which consisted in
discovering and pulling out a plug that released
a door concealing food, and situated in a distant
part of the cage (frontispiece), the correct

performance of the task by a trained monkey
sufficed to attract the attention of another,
previously unsuccessful, animal to the plug;
yet the latter, although pulling out the plug,
failed to appreciate the consequence of his
action, neither going over to the door in search
of food, nor even so much as glancing in its
direction. On the other hand, the same set
of experiments furnishes us with an exactly
contrary instance. A trap door, placed in a
slide (or chute), which when released allowed
food to fall down on to the floor of the cage,
could be worked by the pulling of one of three
strings some short distance away. One monkey,
after showing his inability to solve the problem
unaided, was permitted to see a trained animal
work the mechanism. On the removal of the
latter the first subject at once began to attack
the strings eagerly but indiscriminately, leaving
off repeatedly, despite his non-success, to investi-
gate the food-opening. It seems pretty evident
that, in this case at least, an association had
been definitely formed, though it would appear
to be one of temporal, rather than of causal,
sequence.

Incidentally, it may be noted that, the
experimenter reports not only the act of the

imitatee, 'but also the profitable result of that act was a necessary factor in producing imitation.' Somewhat similar observations have also been made concerning white rats. For Berry found that with these rodents the ' following tendency,' far from being unconditioned, was strictly controlled by the result. Untrained rats on finding that their companions could show them a way of escape would follow the latter about closely, desisting at once, however, if they failed. This, Berry designates as a type of behaviour intermediate between instinctive and intelligent imitation proper.

We have seen how easily movements initiated by playful interest or curiosity, and resulting in a chance success, may be mistaken by a superficial observer for a true instance of reflective imitation. But there is another no less insidious error to be avoided with equal care.

Because an animal fails in an experiment designed to test its ability to imitate, it by no means follows that it is incapable of truly imitative action. It must first be proved that the test set was an appropriate one, suited to the subject.

For instance, before entering upon such

an investigation, it is only methodical to ascertain
that the subject's attention can be readily
aroused through the particular sense avenue
to which appeal is made. Self-evident as this
would seem, it is a precaution that is only too
often overlooked. Nor, even after the most
careful efforts to secure the conditions best
adapted to compel the subject's attention, can
the issue be guaranteed. An animal's attention
is an uncertain quantity, and, at best, seldom
concentrated for long at a time on one object
or situation, except in certain special cases as,
e.g., a cat watching over a mousehole, where,
indeed, the tendency is inherited. Perhaps
something could be done if animals, destined
to participate in experiments on imitation and
kindred inquiries, could be subjected in their
youth to a course of training in the habit of
giving attention. As it is, the actual turning
of the imitator's head or even of his eyes towards
the imitatee's movements are not, in themselves, sufficient assurance that the attention
is caught. Simian attention, in particular, is
of so roving a character as to have given rise
to the assertion that it is impossible to be sure
that an object has been noticed by a monkey
unless he actually touches it.

Allowing for these facts, the large proportion of failures which result when the imitator is confined in a separate compartment from the imitatee ceases to cause surprise; the condition, it will be readily understood, being a most unfavourable one.

It was pointed out above how essential it is to insure that the correct working of a mechanism, consequent upon witnessing its operation by another animal, is not the result of some chance success in which intelligent imitation plays no part; as when the trained animal's movements simply serve to direct the imitator's attention to a hitherto neglected factor in the environment, which is then successfully manipulated in a more or less automatic manner or by some happy accident. And here we are faced with a dilemma. The particular action demanded from the imitator must obviously be one possible for him and not too difficult of execution; otherwise failure may be due to the complexity of the action and not to inability to imitate intelligently where the conditions are favourable. On the other hand, if the movement required is very simple and natural there is always the possibility that its performance is not due to imitation but

has occurred spontaneously or by chance. Nor
does the fact that an animal never hit on
the action in question (at all events in the
right connexion) while alone, but only after
another animal had accomplished it in his
presence, by any means constitute an adequate
safeguard. For, though the number of simple
movements in an animal's *répertoire* is limited,
the order of their appearance is, to a large
extent, haphazard, and thus resort to the suitable
action may have been simply delayed : or,
as we have just seen, while the behaviour of
the imitatee may have been instrumental in
calling attention to the mechanism, the latter
may of itself provoke the appropriate response.
Conditions constituting the *juste milieu* are but
seldom obtained.

As regards the facility with which various
kinds of movements are reproduced, it is generally
agreed that those which are instinctive and
common to the species are the most readily
imitated ; a fact which, if true, goes far to explain
the disproportionately large number of failures
that result when an animal, instead of imitating
the behaviour of another of its own kind, is
required to copy the experimenter.

A propos of exact copying as distinguished

from reflective imitation, an interesting method
has been employed by Porter. The subjects
were birds, comprising several species. Each
bird was allowed to learn to work a mechanism
in its own way; whereupon it was found that
in practically no two cases did the method
adopted agree in every particular. A bird
having learnt to work the mechanism in its
own way was then allowed to see another bird
attack it in the latter's own characteristic
manner. Should the former bird thereupon
modify its behaviour, adopting a procedure
similar to that followed by the second bird,
there would be good reason for supposing the
case to be one of definite imitation. These
experiments also satisfy another condition, that
of securing the subject's interest. For the association between mechanism and reward being
already established, the interest inherent in the
latter will doubtless be irradiated to the former;
while the entrance of the social factor, and with
it rivalry, adds the final fillip. The results are not
altogether clear-cut, for the conditions of the
method which allowed of the free exercise of
rivalry and interest, also led one bird to displace
another at a very early stage of the latter's
efforts. One crow did, however, change his

manner of opening a door, owing, it is claimed, to imitation; the experimenter also asserts that his observations showed that the method under discussion is likewise practicable with orioles and with the junco, the sparrow, and the cowbird.

Concerning the influence of social relations all too little is known. According to Thorndike, on the one hand, we should expect 'members of a common troupe of animals on friendly terms to manifest it [imitation] more than others'; and it is suggested that the negative results of his experiments with monkeys are, in part, to be ascribed to the hostile relations existing between his subjects, two of which were on terms of war and the third extremely shy and timid. Haggerty, on the contrary, as the outcome of his observation of monkeys expresses the opinion that 'familiarity tends to lessen attention, to make each animal follow its own tendencies. Strangeness and a certain amount of pugnacity seem effective in arousing attention,' though fear only causes a monkey to attend to its enemy's movements in so far as may be necessary to avoid him.

Neglect to observe the precautions indicated, together with a tendency to overlook the animal equation and the general conduciveness of the conditions to imitation, in the anxiety to secure a rigorous test, may in part account for the high percentage of failures. On numerous occasions the behaviour of cats, dogs, raccoons, and monkeys alike, has yielded no evidence whatsoever of any imitative ability. Yet, it must be remembered, that even the few tests which may be regarded as approximating, in some measure, to the ideal standard are unable to do more than suggest, though with a very high degree of probability, the presence of intelligent imitation. No case has, as yet, been recorded which cannot, in the last resort, be adequately analysed on the 'stimulus and response' basis, the object or situation, either in itself or through association, suggesting the appropriate reaction. At all events there is no need to postulate ideas as directive of the observed conduct. True, they may be the determinant; but this is a hypothesis that can only claim serious attention, if the general conduct of the subject under consideration is confirmatory of the supposition.

It is clearly impossible, in the limited space at our disposal, to deal in detail with the many investigations that are concerned with the imitative powers of the higher animals. Nevertheless, in view of the prevalent belief in the imitative disposition of monkeys (typified by the verbs 'ape' and '*singer*') this chapter cannot be brought to a close without some attempt to summarise, if only very roughly, the results of actual experiments with these animals.

Within recent years several careful researches —notably those of Haggerty, Hobhouse, Shepherd, Thorndike and Watson—have been directed to the elucidation of this problem : and, thanks to their efforts, we are at last in possession of some data of a reliable character.

Though the results obtained vary somewhat in the different cases, they, nevertheless, all agree in pointing to the conclusion that monkeys are by no means hyper-imitative. Indeed, none of the subjects of Thorndike or Watson—the one experimented with three, the other with four, animals—gave the least evidence, despite abundant opportunity, of any attempt to make intelligent use of imitation : nor did they even manifest instinctive imitation in any marked degree. These facts, while insufficient, as Thorndike admits, to justify a complete refutation of the occurrence of reflective imitation in monkeys, at least prove that the current opinion greatly needs modifying.

Turning to the work of the other three experimenters, each records one or more instances
of partial success, though tempered by many
failures. Between them they tested 21 monkeys,
the majority of which were *Cebus*, *Macacus*
or *Rhesus*.

Haggerty's observations are the fullest. Out
of 26 trials he obtained 16 cases of successful
imitation, 5 cases of partially successful imitation, and only 5 failures. The tests themselves,
two of which have incidentally been already
described (pp. 132–133), involved fairly complex
actions, as is further shown by the following
examples : (*a*) to jump on a chute ; then, swinging head and shoulders down, to thrust up a
hand inside and grasp a coiled spring : this
releases a door through which food falls down
the chute ; (*b*) to climb a rope, push open a
door at the top of the cage and reach for food
placed outside ; (*c*) to push up a screen, or tear
paper, fastened over a circular hole in which
food is concealed.

Hobhouse's experiments differed from Haggerty's in that his animals—a chimpanzee and
a *Rhesus*—were required to imitate, not a fellow-
monkey, but the experimenter. Although the
performance of a human imitatee can scarcely

be considered so likely to induce imitation as that of a member of the same species, Hobhouse is, nevertheless, able to report several successes.

Certain of his tests, *viz.* (1) learning to push out with a plunger a banana wedged in the middle of a glass-tube; (2) learning to use a ⊤-rake to sweep in food placed beyond reach outside the cage, were repeated by Watson, and later by Shepherd. The behaviour described by both these investigators, however, is very different from that of Hobhouse's subjects, though the imitatee was still the experimenter. Watson in every case got entirely negative results, his animals displaying not the slightest tendency to imitate. Shepherd worked with 8 *Rhesus* monkeys, none of which, in the glass-tube test, made any attempt, even after three weeks' experience, to reproduce the movements of the experimenter. In the second test also, six of the subjects again failed. While they learnt to pull in the rake, the action was devoid of meaning since they omitted to hook it first round the food. One monkey, however, did learn, after several days, to accomplish this essential part of the performance, though always in a somewhat clumsy manner. The eighth animal, which had learnt nothing from watching the experimenter, finally acquired the action from another monkey which had just become proficient. The latter was also given a third test. A banana was suspended out of reach, but could be got by mounting a horizontal pole. The pole, however, had first to be brought into position; this could be effected by simply pushing one end along a beam until the pole lay under the fruit, its other end being pivoted. After the experimenter had gone through the performance a few times, the monkey began to copy him. Moreover, Shepherd tells us, that she never 'groped' at all but showed 'an immediate grasp of the situation.' Nor was the action stereotyped, the pole being sometimes pushed, sometimes pulled, but always with the one aim. In short, her behaviour was suggestive of 'imitation of a relatively high order.'

The net outcome of the various inquiries may be stated as follows :—That while under certain circumstances monkeys may, and do, imitate, their behaviour as a whole can scarcely be characterised as imitative ; nor does imitation appear to play any important part in their learning processes.

It is possible that the belief in their imitative powers may have partly arisen from the close resemblance their movements naturally bear to those of human beings, together with their great curiosity, and their manipulative tendencies. Moreover, there are some grounds for supposing that the anthropoids are considerably more imitative than monkeys; but up to the present no systematic investigation has been carried out on the higher apes.

CHAPTER VII

WE have just seen that the interpretation of an action as due to reflective imitation can only be justified if our knowledge of the general level of intelligence manifested by the subject supports the view that, the animal is capable of a type of behaviour higher than that of the mere sensory response, extended though this may be by sensori-motor association. But how, it will be asked, is such knowledge to be obtained? Is there a recognised system of procedure? It must at once be confessed that the ideal method is still to seek. In the meantime it may be of aid to examine the methods now current, noting the points of failure while profiting by the difficulties that have been outgrown.

Thorndike's classical experiments may be said to form the true starting-point of systematic 'intelligence tests.' And, indeed, they are still largely instrumental in determining the methods and character of these investigations. Problem-boxes, some of which were described in the last chapter, and one of which is shown in fig. 9, were the medium chiefly employed. Animals could obtain food or release by a simple action, such as pulling a loop of string or wire,

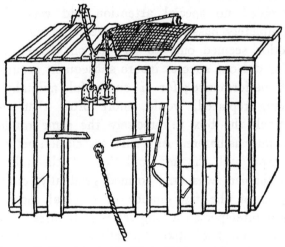

Fig. 9. Problem-box used by Thorndike in experiments on cats. (After Thorndike.)

clawing a button, raising a thumb-latch, raising a lever whilst simultaneously pushing against a door, etc. The mode of attack, rate of learning, and so forth were thought to indicate the nature of the process, revealing whether ideas were active or the formation of a *quasi*-mechanical association alone was involved.

It was found that animals on first being subjected to these tests failed to comprehend the problem. Frantic attempts were made to escape, various parts of the cage being attacked indiscriminately; but the release mechanism received no special attention and was often completely passed over. Indeed, the successful action seemed only to be 'hit on' by chance. Nor did one success insure subsequent accuracy of performance; for a successful animal, on being replaced, would, more often than not, attack the box in precisely the same random manner as before. As a rule, association between escape and the manipulation of the release-mechanism was only formed gradually, on the basis of the few chance or residual successes that interspersed a long series of failures. Such behaviour Thorndike characterises as a 'method of trial and error.' He regards it as non-intelligent, evincing no trace of a directive idea, no perception of the specific relations involved : rather is it akin to the formation of a habit, the successful reaction becoming gradually 'stamped in' by reason of its very success. Thus it comes about that in time the mere sight of the mechanism automatically suggests the movement necessary to effect escape. In short, nothing more is involved than the acquirement of a sensori-motor association.

On such a system of interpretation the importance attached to the curve which graphically represents the learning process in terms of time, will be at once evident. The material from which these curves are constructed is the time taken to escape on each successive trial. Thorndike asserts that 'the gradual slope of the time-curve...shows the absence of reasoning' and further goes on to interpret, somewhat arbitrarily, such a gradual slope as 'representing the wearing smooth of a path in the brain, not the decisions of a rational consciousness'; a view which has since passed current for some years. Recently, however, the admissibility of such an interpretation has been called into question. It appears that the learning curve is a much more complex phenomenon than was at one time suspected, and we are now told, on the basis of subsequent investigation, 'that the rational status of a group of animals cannot be inferred from the slope of a curve in so far as this slope is dependent upon the number of trials or the relative rate of elimination.' Moreover, even in the rare cases where such inferences are legitimate it would seem that 'the relation between the abruptness of slope and degree of rational ability is just the inverse of that assumed by Thorndike.' Other criticisms might also be urged; but those just brought forward will suffice to show the necessity for a review of the evidence contributed by the learning curve.

Although Thorndike argues that the nature of the learning curve may suffice to demonstrate the absence of intelligence, yet he implicitly admits its inadequacy, apart from other sources of information, to establish the converse. Thus while he asserts that the presence of inference, however rudimentary, ought to manifest itself by a sudden vertical descent in the time-curve, he allows that not every such sudden descent implies inference: a marked drop might be due, for example, to the simplicity of the required action. A case in point occurs in the curves constructed by Thorndike from the behaviour of his monkeys. The graphs obtained with these animals differed considerably from those yielded by cats and dogs, 'being unanimous, save in the very hardest, in showing a process of sudden acquisition by a rapid, often apparently instantaneous, abandonment of the unsuccessful movements and a selection of the appropriate one which rivals in suddenness the selections made by human performers.' Yet although Thorndike admits in such a case that it is natural to infer the monkeys come to have an idea of the movement to be made, he hesitates to draw this conclusion. Instead he puts forward various alternative explanations, *e.g.* the superior sight, greater mobility and more dextrous use of the hands by these animals (none of which, it will be noticed, involve the assumption of ideas), to account for the remarkable rapidity of learning.

Thorndike's arguments are not confined to the rate of learning, however. He resorts to many other considerations to support his contention that ideas did not function in the behaviour of his subjects. For instance, his cats and a chick learnt to form non-rational associations in which there could be no perceptible causal relation between means and end, such as that release would follow the action of licking or scratching themselves or in the case of the chick of preening, in very much the same manner and with no greater difficulty than had been shown in mastering the problem-boxes.

Another point upon which he lays great stress is the failure of his animals to learn an action by being 'put through' it. In view of the central part this argument has played in the discussion of the nature of animal intelligence, it must now be examined in some detail. Thorndike noticed that when, preparatory to each new test, his cats were required to go through a door into the trial-box, they formed the habit of entering of their own accord after a certain number of trials. The possibility suggested itself that, the animals might have come to associate the idea of being in the box with the idea of the food that rewarded their escape. In order to put this view to the test, the method of dropping the subjects into the trial-box through a hole in the top was tried with some other cats. None of the animals treated in this manner showed any trace of returning to the box of their own accord though allowed as many trials as the first set of animals. These two cases, Thorndike declares, differ in only one important respect; namely, that whereas the original method allowed of self-initiated muscular innervation, and therefore of the experiencing of impulse, it was of the very nature of the later procedure that it precluded the possibility of experiencing any such

impulse. The same applies to being passively
'put through' the action whose successful performance is necessary to obtain food or release;
no impulse is experienced, and no association is
formed. Whence he concludes that 'the impulse is the *sine qua non* of the association.'
The association in question is not an association
of ideas but an association of sense-impression
with impulse.

Further experiments, conducted to determine
the ability of his subjects to learn from tuition,
or by being 'put through' the action by the experimenter, as well as the failure of the animals
to profit by imitation of a trained animal's
performance, confirmed Thorndike in his view
that association in animals, other than monkeys,
generally involves as an integral constituent
the experience of self-innervation.

But do the facts just related really warrant
the deductions drawn? One point deserves
notice as regards the failure of the cats dropped
into the box to return of their own accord,
and may afford the key to the situation. As
is well known, being dropped through a small
hole is a process deeply distasteful to cat-
nature. And it cannot be too frequently insisted
upon that the congeniality and suitability to

the subject of the appointed task must always be borne in mind in any interpretation of animal behaviour.

Again, raccoons, white rats, and rabbits have all been noticed during the course of experimentation to return of their own accord to boxes in which they were previously deposited by the experimenter. If then this test is to constitute, as according to Thorndike it does, a criterion of the operation of ideas, it follows that in this respect the mental level of the white rat and the rabbit is higher than that of the cat, a conclusion few will be prepared to admit. Hunter, for one, prefers to regard the question of ideas as irrelevant in this connexion; and explains the conduct of his rats by the assumption that the 'constant use of the box as a link in the food-getting series has made it attractive in itself'—otherwise stated, 'the very perception of the box has acquired motive power.'

Turning to the more general arguments from tuition and imitation: it has been shown in the first place that Thorndike's observations, which recorded nothing but failure, do not hold universally. Cole's raccoons certainly profited by being 'put through' the action, and in this way learnt to undo various fastenings.

'Putting through' the required movements is a method extensively used by animal trainers; and is said to be the only way of teaching the essential element in the *saut périlleux* or somersault, for instance. Some monkeys, as we saw in the last chapter, undoubtedly imitate or show capability to learn an action from watching the performance of another monkey or human being.

In the second place, we cannot help asking whether failure to learn by these methods must necessarily be attributed to the absence of ideas? And conversely, must ability so to learn be inevitably interpreted as evidence of their presence? To deal first with the former contention: it can scarcely be considered that an animal held by an experimenter and constrained to make certain movements is in an ideal receptive state; while it may cease to struggle, it remains, in all probability, an unwilling subject. In any case the difference between being put through a movement while forcibly held, and repeating an action voluntarily and without restraint, is enormous.

The case of imitation has already been discussed and the difficulty of insuring attention dwelt upon. When further, it is remembered that not infrequently the imitatee is the experimenter, the number of failures is not surprising: for the movements of a human performer, while they might attract notice, would hardly be likely to furnish the same stimulus to imitation as those of another member of the same species; nor can even careful watching be attributed to attentive observation with the view of reproducing the action in question, but must rather be regarded as due to fear, suspicion or playfulness as the case may be. Non-success therefore seems adequately accounted for on other grounds than that of the absence of effective ideas.

On the other hand, success under tuition of either the 'putting through' or the 'imitative' type may be due simply to the fact that under these conditions the range of interest becomes narrowed and defined; possibly even, attention is attracted to the vital part of the apparatus which is then correctly manipulated either by a happy chance or after a series of trials. Indeed, as often as not the mechanism is worked in a manner different from that taught by the experimenter. Nor is it essential to invoke ideas, for, as was shown above, the majority of cases of successful imitation can be adequately accounted for as a direct response to *present* stimuli.

Without entering into further criticism it should be evident from the points already urged that this class of test, which consists in discovering whether learning takes place in the absence of the experience of a specific impulse to the act in question, is of practically no value as a criterion of intelligence; nor does it, if taken alone, afford any safe clue as to the nature of the conduct exhibited.

Before definitely leaving Thorndike's experiments, certain general disadvantages of the puzzle-box method should be noticed. Not the least of these is that the hungry animal in close confinement is in a mood far from that state of calm collectedness favourable to the scientific examination of a novel situation. Nor should it be lost sight of that though the particular action required may not be strange, yet taken in its new connexion it is, presumably, entirely foreign to the subject, and about as meaningless as a camera or combination letter-lock would be to an unsophisticated Patagonian.

On the other hand, it is interesting to note that those subjects which had had considerable experience of problem-boxes came, in time, to adopt a generalised method of procedure; the scope of their activities was narrowed and

attention was more easily directed to the mechanism, so that new fastenings were dealt with more
promptly and efficiently.

It is impossible, however, to rest content
with conclusions drawn solely from the tests
already described, and we must turn to some
very different examples.

Hobhouse observed behaviour in his monkeys
that strongly suggested the presence of articulate
ideas. By an articulate idea is meant one
' in which comparatively distinct elements are
held in a comparatively distinct relation. Thus,
that a bolt must be pushed back is a crude
idea ; that it must be pushed back so as to
clear a staple, a relatively articulate one, implying
a distinction between the parts of the object
perceived (the bolt and its staples), and an
appreciation of the relation between them.'
The following instances illustrate the apparent
presence of such ideas.

A monkey was accustomed to rake in food
by means of a crooked stick. The latter being
placed out of reach he quickly learnt to use
a smaller stick to draw it in ; whereupon he
would exchange sticks and secure the banana.
When food was placed on a table out of reach
of a small *Rhesus* monkey, kept on a chain,

the animal would drag a box to the table, mount it, and so obtain the booty. A chimpanzee that had been taught to haul into his cage a rope, to the farther end of which his food was attached, never hesitated when the rope was knotted to a staple but at once made 'a "long arm" and reached beyond the knot.' What is remarkable, about these incidents, selected from among several of the same kind, is that in each the subject apparently distinguished the parts of the object before him and appreciated the relation between them. Nevertheless, it must be admitted that numerous failures are recorded; nor have later experimenters met with success on reproducing these conditions with other subjects.

One other interesting point may be touched on here. Hobhouse noticed that his monkeys, in order to obtain some desired end, would readily and of their own accord make use of substitutes very different, both in appearance and mode of manipulation, from the instrument originally employed. Thus, a handle of a skipping rope, a cord and a wire were used in rapid succession by one subject in his attempts to bring an attractive object within reach; none of these proving successful, he finally lassooed it with his blanket and drew it in. In another case a stick, a rope, a box rolled forward and, lastly, a dust-sheet, were each tried in turn. Such behaviour Hobhouse regards as embodying what he terms, a form of 'analogical' extension. It may, indeed, be so; yet we must not lose sight of the fact that monkeys which have learnt with considerable labour to pull a string loop make no attempt to pull a wire loop replacing it, despite their eagerness for the familiar reward. Possibly hyper-excitability alone is sufficient to account for the resort to one method after another. At all events, Hunter considers that the varied modes in which raccoons will attack a fastening—they adopt no stereotyped method, but use either paw indifferently, or even substitute pushing with the nose or pulling with the teeth—denote, in all likelihood, nothing more than 'a random use of acquired co-ordinations,' though at one time such behaviour was taken as affording proof that the subject was 'guided by an idea of what it is setting out to accomplish.'

One subject, namely that of imagery, still remains to be discussed. Attempts have at times been made to ascertain whether images play any part in an animal's mental life. Let us examine two of the more important examples. The first is supplied by one of

Cole's tests with his raccoons. These animals were required to discriminate between two series of colours: in the one, white, blue and red were displayed consecutively; in the other, the end colour of the former series (red) was repeated thrice. A raccoon, if it mounted a box, was fed after the white-blue-red series but not after the red-red-red series; the two series being alternated irregularly. Now since the card immediately preceding the reaction was the same in both cases, Cole argues that if the subjects came to discriminate between the two series, it must be because on the appearance of the final card an image of the colours immediately preceding it was retained in consciousness. As a matter of fact, in course of time, all the raccoons came to make the proper discrimination, and refrained from action when the self-coloured series was given. In the light of subsequent work, however, it seems not improbable that the cards played no part whatsoever in discrimination, which was based instead on the *position* of the lever used to raise the *first* card of a series, and on that alone; a view much more nearly in accord with what is known of the general character of the raccoon's behaviour.

But suppose for a moment Cole's analysis to

be correct, is the presence of images indubitably
proved? To begin with, Cole himself remarks
that he 'never *completely* inhibited the animals'
tendency to start up on seeing white or blue,
which were precursors of the red which meant
food.' That the red was not a neglected factor
of the situation, however, is shown by the fact
that after starting forward at white or at blue,
they would turn back and wait for the red
before finally climbing up. Also when red was the
first card shown the raccoons dropped down from
their attitude of expectancy, in which both front
paws were placed on the board, and glanced
indifferently at the succeeding reds. These facts
lend support to an alternative interpretation.

As is well known association possesses an
irradiative aspect and tends to spread over
an ever-widening area from the immediate
focal centre. It seems therefore not unjust
to suppose that in the case under consideration
food became associated, not only with the red
card as preceded by blue and white, but in
less degree both with blue and with white
directly. If this were so the first card, far
from being indifferent, would induce more or
less strongly an adaptive attitude, a state of
preparedness, which would be confirmed (or

contradicted) by the appearance of the second
card, and eventually discharged into action by
the final card. On such a view there is no
necessity to postulate definite imagery. The
stimuli at the moment, and in the order of their
appearance, produce a certain modification in
the animal's condition; and it is to this modification, which is present at the time of reaction,
rather than to a *tertium quid* in the form of
an image, that we must look as supplying the
true explanation. Nor is there even need to
invoke the aid of association, since it is not
unlikely that the three coloured cards in either
series were never at any time perceived as
distinct elements by the subjects. The two
sequences may only have had meaning as
integrated wholes. In the same way, other
cases put forward as demonstrating the presence
of imagery, where ideas *may* have been present,
can, nevertheless, all be explained in terms of
sensory stimulus and response.

For this reason Hunter was dissatisfied
with such methods and elaborated a new one,
the essential point of which was to *insure* that
'the determining stimulus is absent at the
moment of response.' Should success occur
under these conditions, it can only be due to

the subject developing substitutes which take the place of the absent stimuli as carriers of the needed meaning. Briefly described the method employed was as follows:—The subject was placed in a glass release-box, three of the sides of which each faced a door that could be illuminated at will. Only one door was lighted during a test. After the simple habit of going direct to the lighted compartment had been mastered, the next step was to switch off the light before the door was reached ; subsequently this was done while the subject was still confined in the release-box. The problem that now confronted the subject was to learn to go to the door most recently lighted. Should this be accomplished, it rested with the experimenter to determine how long an interval might be allowed to elapse between the switching off of the light and the subject's release without endangering the number of correct responses. Rats (17), dogs (2), raccoons (4) and children (5) were the subjects employed. These all, save one of the rats, acquired a form of delayed reaction. The maximum delay attained was rats, 10 secs.; dogs, 5 mins.; raccoons, 25 secs., and children, 25 mins.

Now the question arises as to the nature

of the cues relied on for guidance in the absence of the light. Careful controls rule out the possibility that the after-glow of the light, variation of temperature, behaviour of the experimenter or any like feature of the external environment supplied the substitute. On the doors being papered round, each with a grey very different in brightness from that used for either of the other doors, thereby supplying a constant factor, no improvement was detected. An examination into the subjective processes which might be adopted for cues, resulted in the rejection of after-images of the light, learning of the order in which the doors were illuminated, etc. But dependence upon motor attitudes of orientation could not be similarly dismissed; since the evidence established practically beyond doubt that the dogs and rats, so far as successful, depended entirely on the maintaining of a constant orientation towards the door in which the light had appeared, so that on release they headed straight for it. There is no call here for a representative factor.

The behaviour of the raccoons, while it sometimes resembled that of the rats and dogs, was often, like that of the children, of a totally different character, in which orientation could not be discovered to play any systematic *rôle*. Careful examination of the remaining possibilities, resulting in their elimination, led to the conclusion that these last two cases force us to the hypothesis 'that the cue disappears after being aroused by the light stimulus, and is re-aroused in some manner at the moment of release.' The process is reconstructed by Hunter somewhat as follows:—He assumes the existence of three intra-organic tendencies (*i.e.* one towards each door) each of which 'becomes associated during the course of the experiment with some sensory factor connected with the releasing of the animal. Hence the release is a stimulus which tends to arouse all three'; actually, however, the release will revive most strongly, *ceteris paribus*, the tendency most recently active. Such an explanation, it will be noticed, while allowing that the type of function is ideational in character, avoids the difficulties involved in the assumption of images. In this it is in line with modern views which have taught us the existence of imageless thought.

Lastly, two methods elaborated by Yerkes and by van Hamilton, respectively, deserve notice.

Both methods claim to be capable of wide

application. It is urged that they are equally valuable for testing, not only human subjects, whether adult or child, normal or mentally deficient; but also apes, monkeys, horses, pigs, dogs, mice, birds, and the smaller reptiles. In addition to their use for comparative purposes they are also valuable for work with individual subjects.

Yerkes first described the method which he has named 'The Soluble-Problem Multiple Choice Method' (usually referred to as the 'Multiple Choice Method') in a lecture delivered in 1913. It was originated for the purposes of work upon patients in the Psychopathic Hospital at Boston, but its wide applicability was at once evident. The aim of the method is to enable the comparative psychologist 'to present to any human or infra-human subject, no matter what the age, degree of intelligence, or condition of normality, a series of situations increasing in complexity from an extremely simple one to one so intricate that even the most intelligent human subject might spend hours or days in adjusting himself to it.'

The details of the reaction-apparatus employed—such as the material of its construction, the dimensions, etc.—are varied according to the requirements of the class of animals under experiment, but the general plan remains the same in all cases. The number of problem situations which can be presented is very great, but in many instances a few of the simpler problems will exhaust an animal's resourcefulness for the somewhat artificial type of task which it is asked to perform.

The reaction apparatus contains a number of keys, or doors, say nine, which are in a row facing the subject. Any, or all, of these keys, or doors, may be in use, according to the requirements of the test; but in all the simpler tests only adjacent doors, or keys, are employed in any given trial. The actual group of doors used may vary in position and number from trial to trial.

Under these conditions crows, pigs, and monkeys have been presented with two or more of the following problems:—

I. Using a group consisting of from two to five adjacent doors out of the given nine doors, to select the first door on the right from the end of the group;

II. Using a group consisting of from three to nine doors, to select the second door on the left;

III. Using a group consisting of from three

to seven doors, out of the given nine doors, to select alternately the end door on the right and the end door on the left. (With this test the same grouping of doors is presented twice in succession.)

IV. Using a group consisting of either three or five of the given nine doors, to select the middle door of the given group, the group varying in number from test to test.

Yerkes' aim in devising these and similar tests has been to force his subjects 'to select the proper mechanism (*e.g.* the correct door) on the basis of some particular relationship of that mechanism to its fellows, this relationship having been determined upon in advance by the experimenter....Without other aid than his own observation, the subject is expected, from repeated presentation of the...[mechanisms], to discover the essential relation, and to acquire the ability to select the right...[mechanism] with certainty.'

Punishment, together with a food reward, have usually been employed, but these can be left to the discretion of the experimenter.

The types of problems which have so far been solved are not very numerous. Crows and pigs have succeeded in solving problems I and

III. Problem II presented greater difficulty, being perfectly solved only by a young sow, after 390 trials. Problem IV proved incapable of solution when large groups of doors—up to seven or nine—were employed; but the pigs learned to select the middle door when the group of doors did not exceed five. It would be interesting to carry out further experiments to determine more exactly the factors underlying correct choice in this last type of problem, and upon what the limitation of successful reaction depends. Thus the parts played by the number and size of the reaction-mechanisms should be elucidated, and the relative importance of these factors made clear.

The complete solution of a given problem is not however, according to Yerkes, essential to the success of his method. He lays stress particularly on its value as an instrument for analysing the different types of reaction of different individual subjects, and of different classes of animals; and for studying the appearance and disappearance of reactive-tendencies during the course of the experimentation.

This leads us to a consideration of van Hamilton's method, for it was his aim, in an investigation, the results of which he described in 1911, to discover types of reactive-tendencies in different classes of animals.

Despite their close resemblance the two methods differ both as regards their primary aim, and in various subsidiary features. Van Hamilton decided that the most satisfactory method for him to adopt would be to present his subjects with a situation that is, strictly speaking, insoluble. To this end he devised the following apparatus and procedure. The subjects were presented with four doors, each equi-distant from the release-box entrance. One of these was unlocked during each trial, and the same door was never unlocked on two successive trials. The locking device was arranged so that it was impossible for the subjects in the trial box to detect, even by the most thorough-going inspection, which of the four doors was open on any particular occasion. Each door was unlocked twenty-five times out of every hundred trials.

In brief, van Hamilton found that five types of reactive-tendency were exhibited by his various subjects, the latter including human adults, dogs, puppies, mature cats, kittens, and a horse. These tendencies he describes thus:

Type A. *The Rational Inference Tendency.* No effort is made to open the impossible door (*i.e.* successful door on immediately preceding trial). No one of the three possible doors is tried more than once. Only human subjects display this tendency.

Type B. *The Unmodified Searching Tendency.* All four exit doors are tried once each, and in irregular order. This appears to be less common in young animals than in older ones of the same species.

Type C. *The Tendency to adopt Stereotyped Methods of Searching.* This occurs only when door 1 (at the extreme left) or door 4 (at the extreme right) is the unlocked door. The subject then tries doors 4, 3, 2, 1 or 1, 2, 3, 4 in order. This tendency is most frequently shown by monkeys, and seldom occurs in human beings or in adult animals of other species.

Type D. *The Searching Tendency modified by Recrudescent Motor Impulses.* Repeated efforts are made to open a given door, but between each attack upon it an effort is made to open some other door. This tendency is exhibited in the highest degree by adult dogs.

Type E. *The Tendency towards Perseveration of Active Motor Impulses and of Inhibitions.* Under this head are embraced various inappropriate modes of attempted solution, namely:

(i) During a given trial a subject tries a door, leaves it, returns to it, and tries a second time *without having tried any other door.*

(ii) During a given trial a subject attacks a group of two or three locked doors two or more times in a regular order.

(iii) During a given trial a subject, without falling into either of the above two modes of reaction, persistently avoids a given exit-door.

Reactions of this type are found more frequently as we descend the phylogenetic and ontogenetic scale. There are, in fact, certain definite factors which favour the manifestation of Type D, and particularly of Type E reactions. Among these are: (*a*) an inherent primitiveness of reactive equipment, such as is characteristic of the rodent species, or of the young of more highly developed species, or of the mentally deficient among human adults; (*b*) excitability; (*c*) distractibility; and (*d*) feeble responsiveness to the situation which elicits the reaction.

If we compare the Multiple Choice Method of Yerkes with van Hamilton's method of investigating reactive-tendencies we find that the first and most marked difference between them is that whereas the former presents his subjects with a precise and definite problem capable of exact solution, the latter presents a situation that is, at best, capable of partial solution only.

Secondly, van Hamilton's method is less plastic than that of Yerkes. His reaction apparatus contains four doors only, one of which is unlocked on any particular trial. By Yerkes, on the other hand, the number of reaction-mechanisms may be varied within considerable limits, and the size of the group employed at any particular trial is not rigidly fixed.

Thirdly, it is on the whole true to say that van Hamilton's method is of value rather for showing the difference in reactive-tendencies between different phyla, or between different age-groups, than for investigating individual differences. The Multiple Choice Method, on the other hand, seems equally well adapted to the latter purpose as to the former, and its most valuable results will, in all likelihood, be obtained from a detailed study of the behaviour of individuals.

The two methods may be regarded as supplementary. Van Hamilton's procedure is not well adapted for prolonged investigation, but may be excellent for preliminary examination. It has the advantage that attention is not diverted from the actual behaviour of the subject, and concentrated mainly on the final step, the success or failure of the total reaction. Strictly speaking complete success is ruled out of court, and so long as the experiment is properly conducted can be due only to chance. The general situation is therefore, in a sense, less equivocal, and better adapted for comparative work than is the case with the Multiple Choice Method. For with Yerkes' procedure the success which an animal achieves may at different times or in different cases be directed by different factors. And when it is the issue of the reaction that is attracting attention this difference may well escape observation. Thus the Multiple Choice Method demands, if it is to be really valuable, a very detailed and searching analysis of the subject's history and behaviour, and in this way may be regarded as particularly well adapted for the study of individuals.

The feature of Yerkes' method which renders it particularly serviceable for prolonged investigations into the behaviour of the more developed organisms is its plasticity; while its greater simplicity, and readier standardisation of results, make it preferable to the older problem-box method, though it is not altogether free from the defects of the latter. It has already been remarked that van Hamilton's method is by its nature discouraging and must not be long continued, or an animal is liable to become sulky, listless, stale, or careless. Thus the very fact that attention is concentrated upon the reactive-tendencies rather than upon the solution of a problem, though it is an advantage in one sense, may easily become a defect in another. It may even be questioned how far it is wise to subject an animal who is later going to be examined by the Yerkes' test to the van Hamilton procedure.

These considerations all tend to the conclusion that while the Multiple Choice Method may be particularly useful when it is applied to an analysis of individual learning capacity, van Hamilton's tests are especially valuable for the purposes of comparative research, and most of all when an attempt is being made to study the reactive tendencies of different groups of animals.

In one way, however, the Multiple Choice Method itself is not wholly satisfactory as a means of progressively testing ability to respond to a set of increasingly complex situations. A subject that has solved problems I and II must inhibit these acquired reactions before it can *satisfactorily* solve problem IV, and confusion may therefore result at a trial in which it happens that the correct door is also the appropriate one for the solution of an earlier learned problem. For example, in some of three-door settings used for problem IV the correct door happens also to be the second door on the left, and its choice would consequently satisfy problem II equally well, thus tending to reinstate the old habit, and to confuse the learning of the new.

From the evidence set forth in this chapter, it is clear that no set of tests so far devised suffices to establish definitely the presence of 'ideas' in animals, though many point to a high degree of intelligence. Possibly we are on the wrong lines in expecting animal intelligence to follow precisely the human pattern; indeed the results secured from the application of the two methods last described indicate that there may be considerable divergence, though some degree of coincidence is to be found. It is clear that the tests hitherto used fall far short of the ideal, since, despite every effort, they fail to secure for any length of time the animal's keen interest.

To sum up we may say that, it is by no means disproved that animals are intelligent and have 'ideas,' but, save possibly for the single exception of Hunter's method of 'delayed re-

actions,' no test as yet applied completely
excludes the possibility that animal learning is
anything more than a process of association
on the perceptuo-motor level. The one point
that clearly emerges is the need for new methods
of inquiry.

BIBLIOGRAPHY

HOLMES, S. J. *The Evolution of Animal Intelligence.* New York, 1911.

WASHBURN, M. F. *The Animal Mind.* 2nd ed. New York, 1917.

WATSON, J. B. *Behavior.* New York, 1914.

All these volumes contain excellent bibliographies of the subject.

CHAPTER I

BOHN, G. Les Variations de la Sensibilité en relation avec les Variations de l'État Chimique interne. *Comptes rendus de l'Académie des Sciences,* 1912, CLIV. 388.

DAY, L. M., and BENTLEY, M. A Note on Learning in Paramoecium. *Jour. of An. Behav.* 1911, I. 67.

JENNINGS, H. S. *Contributions to the Study of the Behaviour of the Lower Organisms,* Carnegie Inst. of Washington, 1904; *Behaviour of the Lower Organisms.* New York, 1906.

LOEB, J. *The Dynamics of Living Matter.* New York, 1906.

MAST, S. O. The Reactions of the Flagellate, *Peranema. Jour. of An. Behav.* 1912, II. 91.

SCHAEFFER, A. A. Selections of Food in Stentor. *Jour. Exp. Zool.* 1910, VIII. 75.

CHAPTER II

BOGARDUS, E. S., and HENKE, F. G. Experiments on Tactual Sensations in the White Rat. *Jour. of An. Behav.* 1911, I. 125.

BOHN, G. *La Naissance de l'Intelligence.* Paris, 1909.

CARR, H., and WATSON, J. B. Orientation in the White Rat. *Jour. of Comp. Neur. and Psychol.* 1908, XVIII. 27.

DASHIELL, J. F. Some Transfer Factors in Maze Learning by the White Rat. *Psychobiology,* 1920, II. pp. 329–50.

HICKS, V. C., and CARR, H. A. Human reactions in a Maze. *Jour. of An. Behav.* 1912, II. 98.

HICKS, V. C. The Relative Value of the different Curves of Learning. *Ibid.* 1911, I. 138.

HUNTER, W. S. Some Labyrinth Habits of the domestic Pigeon. *Jour. of An. Behav.* 1911, I. 275.

PIÉRON, H. *L'Évolution de la Mémoire.* Paris, 1910.

WATSON, J. B. Kinaesthetic and Organic Sensations: their Rôle in the Reactions of the White Rat to the Maze. *Psychol. Rev.* Mono. Supp. 1907, VIII. No. 2.

WILTBANK, RUTLEDGE T. Transfer of Training in White Rats upon various series of Mazes. *Behav. Mono.* 1919, IV. I.

WYLIE, H. H. An Experimental Study of Transfer of Response in the White Rat. *Behav. Mono.* 1919, III. 5.

CHAPTER III

COLE, L. W. The Relation of the Strength of the Stimulus to Rate of Learning in the Chick. *Jour. of An. Behav.* 1911, I. III.

HOGE, M. A., and STOCKING, R. J. A Note on the Relative Value of Punishment and Reward as Motives. *Jour. of An. Behav.* 1912, II. 43.

LOEB, J. *Comparative Physiology of the Brain and Psychology.* London, 1905.

ORBELI, L. A. Réflexes conditionnels du côté de l'œil chez le chien. *Arch. des Scs. Biol.* 1909, XIV. I and 2.

SELIONYI, G. P. *Contribution to the Study of the Reactions of the Dog to Auditory Stimuli.* Dissertation. St Petersburg, 1907.

YERKES, R. M. *The Dancing Mouse.* New York, 1907. Modifiability of Behaviour in its relation to the Age and the Sex of the Dancing Mouse. *Jour. Comp. Neur. and Psychol.* 1909, XIX. 237.

YERKES, R. M., and MORGULIS, S. The Method of Pawlow in Animal Psychology. *Psychol. Bull.* 1909, VI. 257.

YERKES, R. M., and WATSON, J. B. Methods of Studying Vision in Animals. *Behavior Monographs*, 1911, I. 2.

CHAPTER IV

BOHN, G. *La Nouvelle Psychologie Animale.* Paris, 1911.

BREED, F. S. The Development of certain Instincts and Habits in Chicks. *Behavior Monographs*, 1911, I. No. 1.

CRAIG, W. The Expression of Emotion in the Pigeon, I, The Blonde Ring-dove (*Turtur risorius*). *Jour. Comp. Neur. and Psychol.* 1909, XIX. 29.

CUNNINGHAM, J. T. The Heredity of Secondary Sexual Characters in relation to Hormones. *Arch. f. Entwickelungsmechanik*, 1908, XXVI. 372.

DRIESCH, H. *The Science and Philosophy of the Organism*, II. London, 1908.

HACHET-SOUPLET, P. *La Genèse des Instincts.* Paris, 1912.

HOBHOUSE, L. T. *Mind in Evolution.* London, 1901.

KUHLMANN, F. Some preliminary Observations on the Development of Instincts and Habits in young Birds. *Psychol. Rev.* Mono. Supp. 1909, XI. No. 1, 49.

MORGAN, C. L. *Habit and Instinct*, London, 1896 ; *Instinct and Experience.* London, 1912.

MYERS, C. S. Instinct and Intelligence. *Brit. Jour. of Psychol.* 1910, III. 209, 267.

SHEPHERD, J. F., and BREED, F. S. Maturation and Use in the Development of an Instinct. *Jour. of An. Behav.* 1913, III. 274.

STOUT, G. F. *A Manual of Psychology.* London, 1913, 334.

CHAPTER V

CLAPARÈDE, E. La Faculté d'Orientation lointaine (sens de direction, sens de retour). *Arch. de Psychol.* 1903, II. 133.

CORNETZ, V. La Conservation de l'Orientation chez la Fourmi. *Rev. Suisse Zool.* 1910, XIX, 153. De la

Durée de la mémoire des lieux chez la Fourmi. *Arch. de Psychol.* 1911, XII. 122. Quelques Observations sur l'estimation de la Distance chez la Fourmi. *Bull. Soc. Hist. Nat. de l'Afrique du Nord,* 1912.

HACHET-SOUPLET, P. Quelques Expériences nouvelles sur les Pigeons voyageurs. *VI Congrès International de Psychol.* 1909, 663.

PECKHAM, G. W., and E. G. *Wasps, Social and Solitary.* Boston, 1905.

PIÉRON, H. Du rôle du Sens Musculaire dans l'Orientation de quelques espèces de Fourmis. *Bull. Inst. gen. Psychol.* 1905, IV. 168. Le problème de l'Orientation envisagé chez les Fourmis. *Scientia,* 1911, XII. 217.

SANTSCHI, F. Observations et remarques critiques sur le Mécanisme de l'Orientation chez les Fourmis. *Rev. Suisse Zool.* 1911, XIX. 303.

THAUZIES, A. Expérience d'Orientation lointaine. *Arch. de Psychol.* 1909, IV. 66.

TURNER, C. H. A preliminary Note on Ant Behaviour. *Biolog. Bull.* 1906, XII. 31.

WATSON, J. B. Further data on the Homing Sense of Noddy and Sooty Terns. *Science,* 1910, XXXIII. 470.

WHEELER, W. M. *Ants.* New York, 1910.

CHAPTER VI

HAGGERTY, M. E. Imitation in Monkeys. *Jour. Comp. Neur. and Psychol.* 1909, XIX. 337.

McDOUGALL, W. *Social Psychology.* London, 1908.

PORTER, J. P. Intelligence and Imitation in Birds; a Criterion of Imitation. *Amer. Jour. of Psychol.* 1910, XXI. 1.

SHEPHERD, W. T. Imitation in Raccoons. *Amer. Jour. of Psychol.* 1911, XXII. 583.

WATSON, J. B. *Animal Education.* Chicago, 1903. Imitation in Monkeys. *Psychol. Bull.* 1908, V. 169.

BIBLIOGRAPHY

CHAPTERS VI and VII

COLE, L. W. Concerning the Intelligence of Raccoons. *Jour. Comp. Neur. and Psychol.* 1907, XVII.

HOBHOUSE, L. T. *Mind in Evolution.* London, 1901.

SHEPHERD, W. T. Some Mental Processes of the Rhesus Monkey. *Psychol. Rev.* Mono. Supp. 1910, XII. No. 52.

THORNDIKE, E. L. *Animal Intelligence.* New York, 1911.

CHAPTER VII

GREGG, F. M., and McPHEETERS, C. A. Behaviour of Raccoons to a Temporal Series of Stimuli. *Jour. of An. Behav.* 1913, III. 241.

HUNTER, W. S. A Note on the Behavior of the White Rat. *Jour. of An. Behav.* 1912, II. 137. The Delayed Reaction in Animals and Children. *Behavior Monographs*, 1913, II. No. 1.

VAN HAMILTON, G. A Study of Trial and Error Reactions in Mammals. *Jour. of An. Behav.* 1911, I. 33.

—— A Study of Perseverance Reactions in Primates and Rodents. *Behavior Monographs*, 1916, III. No. 2.

YERKES, R. M. A Study of the Behavior of the Crow, *Corvus Americanus* Aud., by the Multiple Choice Method. *Jour. of An. Behav.* 1915, V. 75.

—— A Study of the Behavior of the Pig, *Sus Scrofa*, by the Multiple Choice Method. *Ibid.* 185.

—— The Mental Life of Monkeys and Apes: A Study of Ideational Behavior. *Behavior Monographs*, 1916, III. No. 1.

INDEX

Actinian, position habit in, 25; hungry, 86

Action system, 92

Adaptation, in Protozoa, 10–11, confused with learning by experience, 17–18; persistence of habit due to slowness of, 27

Aggregation phenomenon, 3, 7

Albino mice (see under Mice)

Amphipod, fallible instinct in, 80, 82

Analogical extension, 160

Andrews, 120

Antagonistic reflexes, 93

Anthropoids, imitation in, 145

Ants, homing of, 106; in *Formicae*, 104, 105, in *Lasius*, 103, 105, in *Polyergi*, 104; reliance on visual ensemble by, 114; use of auxiliary cues by N. African, 104; sense of direction in N. African, 118; solar tropism in, 117; retentiveness in, 102; muscular memory in, 106, in *Aphaenogaster*, 119; fallible instinct in *T. cespitum*, 79, 82; nuptial flight of, 94

Aphaenogaster (see under Ants)

Aporus fasciatus (see under Wasps)

Articulate ideas (see under Ideas)

Association, and meaning, 47; laws of cerebral, 73; irradiative aspect of, 138, 162; fear acquired through, 129; of temporal sequence in monkeys, 133; of impulse and sense-impression, 153; of ideational character, 166; of sensori-motor type, 146, used in problem box habit, 149; in problem box experiments, 148; animal learning due to perceptuo-motor, 178; as explanation of apparent inferential imitation, 140

Associations, formation of, under natural conditions, 99; instinctively used in homing, 100; misleading, in homing, 117; non-rational, 151

Associative memory (see under Memory)

Attention, minimum of, required in labyrinth habit, 38; and fear, 139, 156; and imitation, 133, 135, 137, 155; training of, 135, 158

Attunement, in rhythmical habits, 27; in homing, 102

Auditory discrimination habit in cat, 29

Auditory experience not essential to labyrinth learning in rats, 36

Auditory reactions in dog, 74–75

Auditory stimuli, response of fish to, 52–55

Automata, lower organisms considered as, 3–4

Automatic character, of labyrinth habit, 38–40, 41–42; of positional memory, 110

166; replaced by orientation cue, 165

Imitating instinct, 86, 123, 124

Imitation, instinctive, 122–131, 141; in young animals, 124, 128

Imitation, suggestion, 125, 128; social influence, 125–127

Imitation, educative influence of, 128–130; self-imitation or circular reaction, 130

Imitation, intermediate types of, 126, 134

Imitation, inferential or reflective, 122, 131–145, 146; precautions to be observed in tests on, 132–133, 134–137; conditions favourable to,137, 142; and attention, 134, 137, 155; in monkeys, 141–145; failure to elicit, 134–136, 137, 139–140, 153, 154, 155, 156

Imitation, chance success and, 132, 134, 136, 137; copying, 137–139

Impulse, fundamental in instinct, 88; in homing, 100; essential factor in association, 153; learning in absence of, as criterion of intelligence, 157

Individual differences tested by Multiple Choice Method, 174, 176

Individual experience (see Experience)

Individualised stimuli, no instinctive recognition of, 80

Individuals, examination of (Jennings), 4

Inference, Thorndike's criterion of (see under Criterion)

Inferential imitation (see under Imitation)

Ingenuity, outcome of generalised instincts, 82

Inhibition, in perch, 51–52, and fear, 84; occurrence of, noted by van Hamilton, 172

Inner sense (see under Sense)

Innervation (see Self-innervation)

Insects, 99, 100–101 (see also Ants, Bees, Beetles, Wasps)

Instinct, 77–98; test of strength of, 50; classical view of, 77; and intelligence, 78, 97–98; fallibility of, 78–80, 100–101, 117; generalised nature of, 81–85; impulse essence of, 88; distinguished from reflexes, 78–89; modifiability of, 77, 83–84, 98; and experimentation, 82–83; self-dependent, 89; waning of, 89; and structure, 92–93, 94–97; and practice, 94–97; and imitation, 122, 123–126; imitating, 86, 123, 124; homing, 99, 100; mating, 80; pecking, 123; habit, 97

Instinctive dispositions, condition of functioning of, 90–93

Instinctive imitation (see under Imitation)

Instinctive reaction, inhibition of, in perch, 51–52

Instinctive response, modified by experience, 77, general suitability of, 82, extension of, 85–87; indirect nature of, 88

Instincts, deferred, 93–94; periodic, 91–92; perverted, 89; transitory, 94

ger, 143; 'putting through,'
152–156; rope, 142; screen,
142; T-rake, 143
Tetramorium cespitum (see un-
der Ants)
Thauziès, 116
Theory, trial and error, 9–10,
21–22; tropistic, 4, 9, 10, 13,
21–22
Thermal reactions (see under
Reaction)
Thigmotaxis, 51
Thorndike, 65, 139, 141, 146,
148, 149, 150, 151, 152, 153,
154, 157
Time curve (see Learning curve)
Time record of labyrinth run-
ning, 43–45
Topographical knowledge, 103;
memory, 114–115
Tournoiement de Turner, 120
Trachelomonas, 12
Training, 31, 50–52, 56–60, 71–
72, 108, 135 (see also Educa-
tion, Punishment and Tui-
tion)
Trial and error, method of,
148; theory of (see under
Theory)
Triplett, 51
Tropism, solar, 117
Tropisms, 21, 22, 89; associa-
tive memory not operative
in, 50; theory of (see under
Theory)
Tuition, 153, 154, 155, 156
Turner, 103, 119, 120
Turtles, incentive to habit-
formation in, 31; automatic
nature of labyrinth habit in,
38; slowness of discrimina-
tion in, 50; form discrimination by, 66

Ultra-violet rays, 3
Unconditioned reflex (see un-
der Reflex)
Unknown sense (see under
Sense)
Useful errors, 83

van Hamilton (see Hamilton)
Vibrissae, function of, in labyrinth learning by rats, 36,
37
Vision, function of, in learning
of labyrinths, 36, 37, 38, 40–
41; use of in homing, 101,
aided by flight, 115
Visual cues (see under Cues)
Visual discrimination (see under Discrimination)
Visual memory (see under
Memory)
Visual movement, formation of
conditioned reflex to, 72

Waning of instincts, 89
Wasps, instinct in, 89
Wasps, homing in, 108–109, in
Aporus fasciatus, 108; use of
landmarks in, 108–109, 110;
locality studies by *Cerceris*,
106–107, by *Sphex*, 106–107;
positional memory rare in,
111, found in *Bembex*, 111,
112; sense of direction in
Diamma bicolor, 120
Watson, 36, 105, 141, 143
Waugh, 62
Weber's law, 59, 60
White rats (see under Rats)
Wiltbank, 45
Wind (see under Cues)

Yerkes, 56, 59, 60, 69, 70, 90,
166, 169

For EU product safety concerns, contact us at Calle de José Abascal, 56–1°,
28003 Madrid, Spain or eugpsr@cambridge.org.

www.ingramcontent.com/pod-product-compliance
Ingram Content Group UK Ltd.
Pitfield, Milton Keynes, MK11 3LW, UK
UKHW020316140625
459647UK00018B/1906